THE DEEP END

THE DEEP END

THE LITERARY SCENE IN THE
GREAT DEPRESSION AND TODAY

Jason Boog

OR Books

New York · London

All rights information: rights@orbooks.com
Visit our website at www.orbooks.com

Cover image: Anton Refregier, *Untitled (detail of figure: historic survey panel, mural study, Cultural Activities of the WPA, WPA Building, New York World's Fair, 1939)*, 1939, oil on paper. Washington, DC, Smithsonian American Art Museum.

Excerpts from Edward Newhouse's *You Can't Sleep Here* (New York: The Macaulay Company, 1934) are reprinted with permission of Alison Dinsmore.

Every reasonable effort has been made to contact copyright holders of material excerpted in this book. Questions may be directed to rights@orbooks.com.

First printing 2020

Published by OR Books, New York and London

Library of Congress Cataloging-in-Publication Data: A catalog record for this book is available from the Library of Congress.

Typeset by Lapiz Digital.

paperback ISBN 978-1-935928-91-1 • ebook ISBN 978-1-68219-217-7

CONTENTS

INTRODUCTION
The Green New Deal

"Somehow," wrote Aubrey Williams in a 1936 *New York Times* essay, "we do have to convince millions of our young people that we have not yet come to a social doomsday, and that there is something better for them to do than jump off the deep end—a phrase common among them which apparently covers everything from the lawlessness to resignation, despair and even suicide."[1] Williams was the director of the New Deal's National Youth Administration, but he had worked as a social worker, as a preacher, and as the publisher of *The Southern Farmer*, a weekly newspaper in Alabama. The phrase "jump off the deep end" held a dark power throughout his essay, evoking the brutal force of the Great Depression.

That quote preoccupied me as I finished this book during the COVID-19 crisis of 2020 and the world felt the tug of the deep end once again. In just five weeks, 26 million Americans filed for unemployment, following a cascade of national shelter-in-place orders. Nothing can capture all the sadness and pain wrapped inside that statistic. At the darkest moment of the Great Depression, unemployment in the United States peaked at 24.9 percent, but economist Miguel Faria-e-Castro predicted we could yet see a 32 percent unemployment rate[2] as this singular disaster unfolds.

Writers are particularly vulnerable to this crisis. I began writing this book more than a decade ago as a younger journalist covering the publishing beat. From the Great Recession onward, I've written about new problems every single year, watching publishing imprints shutter, seeing federal funding for the arts dry up, and looking on as the ability of a writer to make a living continues to decline.

A wave of firings and consolidation in 2018 highlighted the particular weaknesses of our new media economy. The problems began in November, with Mic—a video driven news organization that once seemed like the future of journalism—getting sold (with massive layoffs) to Bustle Digital Group. Mic publisher Cory Haik departed when the news broke about the closures. She described the twenty-first-century struggle in her farewell letter: "Our business models are unsettled, and the macro forces at play are all going through their own states of unrest . . . if anyone tells you they have it figured out, a special plan to save us all, or that it's all due to a singular fault, know that is categorically false."[3]

During this same period, more major publications laid off staff around the country, such as Vox Media (5 percent of staff cut), Vice (15 percent of staff cut), Refinery 29 (10 percent of staff cut), and Vocativ (entire editorial staff cut). All these publications had seemingly emerged from the wreckage of the Great Recession, only to stumble as ad revenues dried up and unrealistic growth expectations throttled the media industry. "To drive faster growth, they have to charge customers less (increasing demand) and pay workers more (increasing supply), then fill the gap with venture capital funding," wrote Alexis

C. Madrigal in *The Atlantic*.[4] Those venture-capital growth expectations have collided with the realities of a post-pandemic economy. The deep end has been there for years, waiting for us.

Williams and his generation architected the New Deal, an economic stimulus plan that helped jumpstart a wrecked country. Among other things, this book will show how that legislation affected the lives of American writers in the 1930s. If we ever hope "to convince millions of our young people that we have not yet come to a social doomsday" in the twenty-first century, we must begin with the stories of the men and women who survived the Great Depression. As we confront the COVID-19 pandemic, climate change effects, economic inequality, and the poisonous return of nationalism, many are wondering if our country still possesses the will or ability to muster such a radical solution as the New Deal.

We do at least have one response.

"Today is a big day for people who have been left behind,"[5] said Congresswoman Alexandria Ocasio-Cortez in February 2019, unveiling the Green New Deal, a resolution that includes calls for new environmental standards, the accelerated elimination of fossil fuels, the creation of millions of new jobs, and a push for job security and benefits for all citizens. The Green New Deal is a legislative moonshot that gives us one last chance to avert the worst-case scenario for climate change and cope with coming economic disasters.

The then twenty-nine-year-old congresswoman championed progressive policies in her 2018 campaign that unseated a New York incumbent. Ocasio-Cortez co-wrote the resolution with her liberal cohort of newly elected representatives. She would be cheered and ridiculed for the audacious plan that she outlined in her speech:

> Today is the day that we truly embark on a comprehensive agenda of economic, social, and racial justice in the After a decade of economic patches and Band-Aids, the Green New Deal was a real attempt to propose legislation on a scale comparable to the legendary work of the original New Deal.[6]

The Green New Deal's vision has never been more urgent. An entire generation of students and recent graduates are sheltering-in-place as I write this, and millions of young adults are coming of age in an economic vacuum. They will emerge into an unimaginable new world reshaped by the pandemic and the mass closures of businesses in every sector. As Williams told us nearly eighty years ago, we must "convince millions of our young people that we have not yet come to a social doomsday." We must find some measure of hope for their future. And yet, no generation has ever faced this particular combination of circumstances.

Just like Williams' generation did in the 1930s, we need to imagine a solution that is equal to our post-pandemic problems. In an interview with *The Nation*, author Naomi Klein defended the dream of comprehensive climate change action, comparing the Green New Deal with "its only real historical precedent," the original New Deal. Klein sketched out the path to achieving the critical mass that activists gained during that turbulent decade:

> . . . the political dynamics that produced the original New Deal were not a benevolent politician handing reforms down from on high, from the goodness of his heart. Of course, it mattered to have FDR in power instead of Herbert Hoover, but it mattered even more to have an organized population which was flexing its muscles in every conceivable way in the 1930s—from sit-down strikes in auto plants, to shutting down the ports on the West Coast, to shutting down entire cities with general strikes. And it mattered also to have more radical voices who were calling for more radical policies than the New

"We must be as ambitious and innovative in our solution as possible." Representative Alexandria Ocasio-Cortez (center) introduces the Green New Deal in 2019. Photo courtesy Senate Democrats/Flickr.

> Deal was offering, like a truly cooperative economy. All of
> that created the context in which FDR was able to sell the
> New Deal to elites. They were grudging about it, but the
> alternative seemed to be political revolution.[7]

Klein ended the interview by setting a condition. A Green
New Deal could only happen with a "huge grass roots mobili-
zation," a radical recalibration of the way every industry thinks
about labor—from fast-food restaurants to tech companies to
media outlets. Everyone, she wrote, needs to imagine "what
would a Green New Deal mean for us."

By revisiting the stories of how writers survived that
awful time, we can join this all-important work of envision-
ing how a Green New Deal could change our lives in the
twenty-first century. Sheltered-in-place with my family in
2020, I began reading like a time traveler, excavating more
books, newspaper clippings, magazines, and poetry from the
Great Depression. No literary map exists for this territory we
now inhabit, but I kept returning to the work of writers who
survived the economic upheaval of the 1930s.

At a time when I couldn't read the news or my social
media feeds anymore, I wandered deeper inside a labyrinth of
80-year-old sadness and pain. I cannot imagine what the future
will look like even a few days into my own future, much less
one year or ten years from now when my children are grown-
ups. But in these long forgotten books, I found a fragile and
golden thread that helped guide me through our new darkness.

We must reimagine everything again in our own time,
and the lives of these Great Depression writers are a good
place to start. They faced apocalypse and they endured.

Let's follow their stories together, looking for hope or
survivors.

1. EDWARD NEWHOUSE

When the stock market crashed in 2008, the offices closed at the legal publication where I worked. I lost my benefits, my office space, and my security, all in a single meeting. I holed up in the New York University Bobst Library for a couple of weeks as a freelance writer, scribbling reports and watching my health insurance expire. I was a single speck in a national catastrophe for writers.

According to the Department of Labor, the printing and traditional publishing sector shed well over 134,000 jobs during the Great Recession. This was part of a much larger set of losses as digital technology disrupted traditional publishing. Between 1998 and 2013, the book publishing industry lost 21,000 jobs, periodical publishing cut 56,000 jobs, and the newspaper industry shed a staggering 217,000 jobs.

After my old job folded, I camped out on the seventh floor of the library, tucked away among the American Literature shelves. I started looking for clues on how writers survived the Great Depression. In the stacks, I found *You Can't Sleep Here*, a novel written in 1932 by a twenty-year-old Hungarian immigrant named Edward Newhouse. His book tells the story of a young newspaper reporter fired during the early days of the Great Depression who sleeps in a tent city along the East River, and who showers in a bathroom at the New York Public Library.

The reporter paces up and down the side of Central Park at sunrise, hoping to get the first look at the want ads before thousands of other unemployed people. "I had to walk till 55th Street before one of the newsstand men would let me look into the want ads."[1] A quiet desperation permeated every line of Newhouse's story. I couldn't stop reading.

US unemployment peaked at 25 percent while Newhouse was writing his novel. Economic catastrophe led to the unprecedented closing of hundreds of magazines and newspapers. Library budgets were slashed. Chicago and Philadelphia both reported that their book buying budgets had been completely cut for 1933. The NYPL saw its budget cut from $256,000 to $120,000 in the same year.

I came across a photograph of a line outside a Depression-era employment agency. The men were wearing suits left over from better times, waiting in an endless chain. They were resigned souls shuffling towards a wall covered with job posters that had already been filled. A *New York Times* columnist poked fun at the plight of struggling authors in a 1931 column called "Our Lazy Writers": "Our younger writers, possibly due to the greater rewards of success, make a great how-de-do about turning out a fairly long novel once every two years; and for this they must have European trips, winters in California and Florida, summers in Vermont and Maine, city penthouses and what not . . . Can it be that American authors waste too much time attending literary teas?"[2]

"Anybody who really wants to work can find a job." Unemployed men huddle around job posters outside a Sixth Avenue employment agency in December 1937. Photograph by Arthur Rothstein, courtesy the Library of Congress.

In *You Can't Sleep Here*, the novel's young hero struggles to make a living as a writer. "The story sounded funny but the situation wasn't," Newhouse wrote, as his hero finishes yet another story he can't publish. One character chides the young journalist: "Anybody who really wants to work can find a job,"[3] and you can feel Newhouse's fury radiating through the pages.

"Anybody who really wants to work can find a job." The old lie is still alive. Internet job boards have created the illusion of boundless opportunity during our Great Recession, but I soon came to realize, like everybody else, that automatic email programs did most of the responding. This was new corporate machinery to avoid discrimination lawsuits and to create the illusion of agency and opportunity. I read a story about a thousand people applying for a minimum wage job at some online publication. It was easy to imagine us all as that throng of unhappy men in the Great Depression photograph, shuffling toward some imaginary goal.

Scattered among those job postings were the realities of the gig economy. Apps had broken transportation, food delivery, and housecleaning into discrete units that could be performed by temporary workers around the country. In a quest for endless growth, these companies turned to automated strategies to find gig-based employees. For a year straight, I received a stream of job emails promising to "Supplement Your Writer Income." These job postings had nothing to do with writing. They were part of an enormous automated campaign to find more Uber drivers around the country, feeding the same subject line to writers who couldn't make ends meet anymore. These job descriptions had nothing to do with expertise in the field: "Drive with Uber and earn money anytime it works for you. Driving is an easy way to earn extra, and it's totally flexible around your schedule. You decide when and how much you drive."

This "Supplement Your Income" recruitment strategy also worked for Postmates, a food delivery company that depends on a fleet of gig-economy drivers. That company flooded job sites with automated and generic job postings with the same structure: "Teacher? Earn Extra Income—Drive for Postmates!" There were hundreds of postings targeting everybody in our gutted workforce with the same "Earn Extra Income—Drive for Postmates!" structure: Receptionist? Maintenance Technician? Social Worker? Medical Technician? Administrative Assistant? Call Center Representative? Registered Nurse? The flurry of job title queries highlighted the fractured state of our post-recession economy. Millions of workers needed to supplement lower paychecks with gig-economy work.

As more and more workers have turned to the gig economy, transportation earnings have steeply declined. The JPMorgan Chase Institute published a 2018 report about the state of our "online platform economy," analyzing how 2.3 million Chase checking accounts processed gig-economy earnings—crunching 38 million payments directed through 128 different online platforms from 2012 to 2018. During that period, "transportation sector" gig-economy drivers for companies like Uber or Postmates saw earnings decrease by 53 percent.[4] The gig economy gave our post–Great Recession economy the illusion of progress, but we filled the landscape with unreliable jobs offering diminishing pay.

We officially emerged from our nationwide recession in 2009, but the situation facing contemporary writers has not changed. The newspaper and magazine jobs that disappeared were never replaced. The bookstore chain Borders closed for good in 2011, erasing nearly 10,700 bookselling jobs. The American Library Association noted that 55 percent of urban libraries, 36 percent of suburban libraries, and 26 percent of rural libraries cut their budgets in 2011. In the same survey, librarians said that job-search services were most in demand at the library, but that 56 percent of the libraries didn't have enough resources to meet the demand.

Wherever I looked, I discovered that Newhouse had been there before me, describing what he called "the crisis generation":

> I was the crisis generation who had never been absorbed into the industry or the professions. Depression. Periodic dip. Economic cycle. Normal course of events. Aftermath of speculation. Act of God. We had all the old problems . . . but we also had something new, the passing of economic insecurity. We college and high school and public-school graduates were certain of our economic future. The pile of lumber and the cement under the billboards was [our] immediate future. The public comfort station down the block and leftover buns at the automat and hourly supervision by twirling bats were our certainties.[5]

The Crisis Generation. That phrase guided me through the next few years. I paid fifty dollars to get a copy of Newhouse's out-of-print novel so I could show it to everybody I knew. Like some misguided missionary, I'd wave it around and say, "See? See? He's talking about us!" His book felt like a bomb with a busted timer that had stalled back in the 1930s and had been stuck on a dusty shelf for eighty years, losing none of its dangerous potency. I wanted to fix the timer and blow something up all over again.

Even so, researching these pages, I saw the tremendous class privilege that helped me survive this long as a writer. As a white man from a middle-class family, I had a certain level of security and privilege, a safety net that cushioned me from the worst parts of the recession. Even though I chose a turbulent profession, I fared far better than millions of Americans who lacked my opportunities. Robert Frank described this privilege in his 2009 *New York Times* essay, "Before You Protest, Thank Your Lucky Stars." He wrote: "People born with good genes and raised in nurturing families can claim little moral credit for their talent and industriousness. They were just lucky."[6]

Throughout the Great Recession, the media industry depended on the work of writers of privilege. In a 2016 interview, Shane Smith, executive chairman of Vice Media recalled the early days of his digital publication: "There was a time when we were a trustafarian commune, and that was fun, that was good,"[7] he reminisced. The Urban Dictionary defines trustafarians as "privileged white kids who subscribe to the hippie lifestyle (because they can) since they have no worries about money, a job etc."[8] Built by these industrious upper-crust workers, the company's value has since ballooned as high as $5.7 billion and now pays top salaries.

I never enjoyed a trustafarian lifestyle, but I survived the recession with a series of steady writing jobs—including an unpaid internship at a glossy magazine. How many writers missed crucial digital journalism opportunities because they lacked the financial security required to enter the profession?

In 1938, a book called *New York Panorama* captured a similar calculus that took place during the Great Depression:

> The few writers who starved it out until fame reached their garrets have been memorialized in many romantic biographical sketches; but of the many who were forced by want to abandon their literary aims no record exists. In New York City, where struggling authors are to be found in greater numbers than anywhere else in the country, the depression of the early 1930's had unusually severe effects, and there was a united demand that the Federal government should include in its work-relief program a plan to employ the writer in work suited to his training and talent.[9]

My book is dedicated to the stories of poets, novelists and journalists who never made it. My bookshelves have always been filled with underdogs, because I still remember the uncertainty of my early days as a writer. Our canon should celebrate more than just the lucky few writers who managed to survive the Great Depression with their reputations and lives intact. We should remember the writers we left behind.

The New Masses

Alison Dinsmore, the daughter of Edward Newhouse, sent me a photograph of her father. Newhouse looks sly in the picture. His fedora is tipped at a hard-boiled angle. His trenchcoat collar is popped up to keep out the cold. He peers over his shoulder. He is the scrappy reporter already looking out of the frame for the next story. He does not smile, instead keeping his mouth tight and serious.

Henry Ford drove Newhouse crazy. The young novelist spent his early twenties hanging out with literary Communists around the city, and the capitalist icon became a clear Depression-era target. The Depression was Ford's opportunity to build an automobile empire on the backs of a non-unionized workforce.

While writing *You Can't Sleep Here*, the young reporter stewed over a newspaper clipping that he saved from 1928. As the American economy unraveled, the European press confronted the automobile mogul. Ford laughed off a question about reports of breadlines in America: "It is curious that we do not hear these things in the United States . . . If there were bread lines, they must have sprung up since I left New York six days ago." Newhouse used an excerpt from that same newspaper article as the epigraph for his novel, a quote describing the celebrity industrialist and his wife dancing on a cruise ship bound for Europe: "Seizing his wife around the waist, Mr. Ford led off with a waltz and everybody joined in . . . "[10]

The rich danced while the workers paid the price.

The hero of Newhouse's book is Eugene Marsay, a name that combines two characters from novels by Honoré de Balzac. Eugene was based on Eugene de Rastignac from *Le Père Goriot*, a bold student in Paris who had a "desire to fathom the mysteries of an appalling condition of things, which was concealed as carefully by the victim as by those who had brought it to pass."[11] Henri de Marsay, on the other hand, "was aristocratic, a noble, a dandy, dauntless, highly skilled, fearless. In Hungarian, [Marsay] is a highly aristocratic name."[12]

Sharing characteristics of both Balzac characters, Eugene Marsay is a member of the newly unemployed middle class, struggling to understand how these "appalling" changes have occurred in America.

When Franklin Roosevelt took office in March 1933, he deconstructed Ford's argument in a remarkable speech. His inaugural address blamed failed banking leadership, unjust distribution of national resources, and ruthless businessmen for the Great Depression. He made an urgent plea that still resonates in our own time:

> The rulers of the exchange of mankind's goods have failed, through their own stubbornness and their own incompetence, have admitted their failure, and abdicated. Practices of the unscrupulous money changers stand indicted in the court of public opinion, rejected by the hearts and minds of men. True they have tried, but their efforts have been cast in the pattern of an outworn tradition. Faced by failure of credit they have proposed only the lending of more money. Stripped of the lure of profit by which to induce our people to follow their false leadership, they have resorted to exhortations, pleading tearfully for restored confidence. They know only the rules of a generation of self-seekers. They have no vision, and when there is no vision the people perish.[13]

The line which is remembered from Roosevelt's speech today is, "The only thing we have to fear is fear itself," but the president also called for new business ethics, job reform, and redistribution of resources. "The joy and moral stimulation of work no longer must be forgotten in the mad chase of evanescent profits," he said, chastising Henry Ford and his cohorts.

Newhouse finally found a job in the summer of 1933. A magazine called *The New Masses* assigned the broke young reporter several stories. First published in 1926 and running until 1948, *The New Masses* was an early outlet for radical writers and unionized workers, featuring some of the most famous voices to emerge from the Great Depression, including Upton Sinclair, Richard Wright, and Langston Hughes. While the journal began as a monthly, it would become a weekly paper during the Depression in an ambitious attempt to reach a new generation.

For an early assignment, the magazine sent Newhouse into the hellish depths of the Commodore Hotel to cover a service worker strike. At the time, the luxury hotel was the biggest in the Grand Central neighborhood, counting two thousand rooms and twenty-eight stories. The hotel staff toiled in an underground complex five stories deep. Subway trains rattled by alongside them. The owners installed a mammoth air-conditioning system, a modern wonder that cooled patrons on the floors above ground. However, in the bowels of the hotel, the cooling system pumped deadly gases straight into the unventilated laundry complex. Newhouse met two women who had collapsed on the laundry floor after inhaling fumes. The foreman brought them upstairs until they recovered consciousness and then sent them straight back down to the machinery.

Newhouse railed against a world where a hotel worker made $1.25 a day while nearly choking to death on coolant fumes. One foreman made a point of lurking around the bathrooms, bursting in when his female employees stayed past the five-minute break limit. Newhouse called it the "merciless speedup."[14]

Companies in the twenty-first century have been adopting similar "speedups": trimming salaries, breaking unions, and pushing for longer hours, capitalizing on the floundering economy. A 2011 investigative report in *The*

Morning Call shed light on punishing conditions inside an Amazon warehouse in Pennsylvania:

> Workers said they were forced to endure brutal heat inside the sprawling warehouse and were pushed to work at a pace many could not sustain. Employees were frequently reprimanded regarding their productivity and threatened with termination, workers said. The consequences of not meeting work expectations were regularly on display, as employees lost their jobs and got escorted out of the warehouse . . . During summer heat waves, Amazon arranged to have paramedics parked in ambulances outside, ready to treat any workers who dehydrated or suffered other forms of heat stress. Those who couldn't quickly cool off and return to work were sent home or taken out in stretchers and wheelchairs and transported to area hospitals. And new applicants were ready to begin work at any time.[15]

Amazon reformed its warehouse policies after this story broke, but it raised a difficult question for activists: how do you fight an online retailer? In 2011 and 2012, the nonprofit *American Rights at Work* staged a Cyber Monday boycott attempting to sabotage Amazon's crucial holiday sales. The group described working conditions in Amazon's fulfillment centers:

> Workers in shipping centers who fulfill online orders are asked to grab items for boxes at unsustainably high speeds. In many cases, workers are required to collect 1,200 items in a 10-hour shift, or one item every 30 seconds. If employees can't keep up, they are disciplined or fired . . . Workers have to continuously cross great distances inside the massive warehouses. 'Pickers,' who locate and collect items for shipping, reportedly walk on average between 12 and 15 miles every shift. Despite some items being football fields apart, workers are expected to maintain the same frenzied pace.[16]

Amazon entered these national controversies with a powerful advantage: they have no physical store locations that activists can target at the height of the holiday season. Protestors cannot reach the customers they wish to confront. Allentown, Pennsylvania's newspaper, *The Morning Call*, covered the boycott in 2011, estimating that Amazon lost 12,600 customers during the action, which cost the online retailer $9 million. Those protests barely dented Amazon's holiday sales. In January 2013, the company noted that net sales had increased 22 percent during that period—totaling a whopping $21.27 billion for the fourth quarter of 2012.

In the 1930s, the Food Workers Industrial Union represented hundreds of Commodore Hotel employees, launching what Newhouse called a "venomous, bitter and desperate strike" that dragged on for ten weeks in the streets of New York City. The union relief committee could only feed the unpaid strikers with dry bread. Newhouse stalked the picket line outside the Commodore Hotel, growing angrier and angrier as he walked: "[Strikers] appear each day with hundreds of other workers who are getting their first glimpses into the magnificent tropical lobby of the bull-necked business men whose linen they launder in the subterranean inferno."[17] Newhouse recorded hotel detectives and cops beating strikers senseless. His prose smoldered with rage. He was a young writer finding his voice during an American disaster.

By August, Newhouse had also landed a gig writing a sports column for *The Daily Worker*. This labor magazine was two years older than *The New Masses* and was founded by American Communists in Chicago. The editors moved the paper to New York City in 1927. With income from both papers, Newhouse scraped together a living.

Newhouse described himself as a radical during these early years:

> as far back as I can remember I have been accustomed to think of myself as a Communist ... The great part of my activity in the Communist movement has been literary. Alternately I worked on the staffs of the Labor Research Association, *The New Masses* and *The Daily Worker*. I was a charter member of the first John Reed Club which started in 1930.[18]

One day, after reporting on the ongoing tribulations of the workers outside the Commodore Hotel, Newhouse toured its upper reaches with a chubby wool-manufacturing executive who was there for an industry conference. While strolling past "tropical birds, the ornate vases, jewelry shop," the mogul complained that his daughter had bought $9,000 in dresses during a recent trip to Europe. "The girl has to be taken in hand," he said. Pausing to buy a stuffed rabbit for her, he told Newhouse to forget about the strikers: "Don't pay any attention to them . . . I don't. Those people don't know when they are well off."[19]

Publishing's First Strike

Within a year, the New York City strikes had spread from farmers to factories. Service workers and even white-collar workers were ready to strike. In June 1934, Newhouse joined a ragtag group of employees from the Macaulay Company, marching in one of the first publishing-industry strikes. Camped out at Fourth Avenue and Twenty-Seventh Street, the picket line protested the firing of a bookkeeper and Office Workers Union member. Eleven employees walked out, making a very public scene in the crowded neighborhood. The strikers had a long list of demands, some of which reveal how rudimentary working conditions were compared to today:

1. All abuse and tyranny on the part of the employers must stop.
2. Employees must be permitted the use of sufficient electric light.
3. The installation of electric fans in warm weather.
4. Employees absent because of illness for a period up to ten days should receive full pay.
5. No discharge without either two weeks' notice or one week's salary.
6. Workers employed by the company for a year or longer should receive two weeks' vacation.[20]

L. F. Furman, the president of Macaulay, blamed the firing on "economy and efficiency," and said he would never take the bookkeeper back. At the end of a *New York Times* article about the afternoon strike, Furman threatened to "re-staff" if the demonstration didn't end soon. He would be in for a long, long summer. The next day, the picket line swelled to thirty-six writers. A thicket of protesters blocked Fourth Avenue foot traffic and attracted swarms of reporters. The cops showed up and got drawn into an argument with a Guggenheim fellow about blocking the street. Shortly after, the police trucks arrived, hauling away eighteen writers including a *New Republic* editor and a *New Masses* editor, Mike Gold.

The poet and novelist Maxwell Bodenheim had once held publishing contracts at Macaulay. He described the publisher's neighborhood in his novel, *Slow Vision*:

> Madison Square Park and its environs showed neither brightness nor comradeship. People flew along, looked at one another with suspicion, or aloofness. A frowning exhaustion was on most of the faces and many of the others—faces of drones, or worldly men and women in good clothes—were inordinately self-centered and showed not a scrap of interest in the human beings passing them.[21]

The police shipped the writers and editors they arrested to Yorkville where they spent two hours in jail, singing "The Star-Spangled Banner" together in the cells before being brought to court. A cop explained that the protesters had peacefully occupied the street with no pushing or shoving, and then the judge sent everybody home. They left a pile of cardboard signs on the courtroom floor. The next day, the protest swelled, with twenty-three more protestors arrested after a long day on the picket lines, including an editor, a publicist, and an actress. This was the last straw: a lawyer showed up and negotiated a truce between Macaulay and the Office Workers Union.

Everybody knew the Depression-era excuse of "economy and efficiency": it justified mass firings and all sorts of workplace abuses. With unemployment at twenty-five percent, employers could manipulate workers with ease. The publisher knew he had workers by the throat. As a testament to his power, only half the staff at the small company had even gone on strike while the other half kept working. The company quickly hired temporary workers from the sea of the unemployed to fill the strikers' spots.

***

The whole time I struggled to make it as a working writer, I was constantly aware of how many people were willing to do the same work I was doing and how many of them would write for free. We were an unlucky generation, squeezed between technological change and economic collapse. We had no place to go, and no bargaining chips. In 2002, 10 percent of the traditional publishing industry was represented by unions, according to the Bureau of Labor Statistics. By 2012, only 4 percent of all employees had union support.

The aughts peeled back more layers of legal protections and workplace rights—taking us back to Depression-era conditions. By prioritizing "continuing to work" over taking a stand on pay and conditions, we all contributed to this new reality. I have never wanted to do anything else with my life except write. I fought bitter battles to hold on to my small corner of the publishing world while trying to ignore the ways in which we are all accountable for the state of the industry in which we work.

***

In September of 1934, the president of Macaulay fired three union leaders working at his publishing house, setting off an even larger wave of protests. Edward Newhouse joined the demonstrations once again. The strike committee telegram was sent directly to President Roosevelt and read: "we earnestly call upon you to enforce your guarantee to the workers of this country."[22] Within days, other writers called for a boycott of the publisher. The famous radical novelist John Dos Passos wired his own support from Los Angeles, attaching the signatures of thirteen other authors: "We urge all writers to refuse to adapt Macaulay books for the screen and to have no dealings with your company until the writers fired for union activity are reinstated."[23]

In a display of cross-industry solidarity that seems unimaginable in today's business climate, employees from all around the city joined the Macaulay strikers, including publishing professionals from Macmillan, Vanguard Press, Charles Scribner's Sons, and The Viking Press. In a *New York Times* interview, Macaulay insisted it wasn't his fault: "We are all in the same boat . . . the depression gives me no choice but to cut my staff. My position is no different from that of other employers who have had to do the same unfortunate thing."[24]

The situation at the company did not improve. Macaulay fired four more union workers and refused to budge when workers launched a second strike in September. The New York Regional Board ruled in the workers' favor, but the publisher successfully appealed to the National Labor Relations Board. The federal decision eventually ruled that since the strike happened before the National Recovery Act was established, the rules preventing employers from firing labor organizers had no authority over the publisher.

Macaulay won in court, but the damage had already been done. Writers now knew they could stand up and fight. *The New Masses* was enthusiastic: "it was the first strike in publishing history. It destroyed forever the notion that white-collar workers are constitutionally averse to using the tactics of the more class-conscious manual workers."[25] *The New Masses* began investing in strike coverage, hiring Newhouse to cover the growing unrest in New York City.

Proletarian Literature

Joseph Freeman, the editor of *The New Masses*, praised Newhouse's novel *You Can't Sleep Here* for its focus on "unskilled intellectuals" like newspaper reporters and other "wage slaves of capitalist arts and letters." In his review, he described a dilemma familiar to bloggers, citizen journalists, and other internet artists:

> . . . in the best of times, such members of the intelligentsia are migratory workers; they drift from jobs; they have neither the training nor the stability of engineers, physicians, lawyers or scientists. They are the first to be declassed by the crisis and pushed into the ranks of the proletariat. In times like these, it means into the ranks of the unemployed proletariat.[26]

Newhouse literally camped out among the "unemployed proletariat" in an East River Hooverville, one of several tent cities scattered around New York City—encampments nicknamed after President Herbert Hoover who oversaw the economic crash of 1929. The homeless men drew water from a fire hydrant two hundred yards away from the camp, carrying drinking water in pots, pails, buckets, and cups back to their shacks. Firewood was currency, scavenged inside the biggest city in the United States. Men pushed baby strollers full of firewood around town, selling kindling and earning half a dollar a day.

A *New York Times* investigative report about Hoovervilles counted some 2,000 men, women and children living in tent cities inside New York City. The reporter found homeless veterans, actors, boxers, mechanics, and workers of every stripe. When a family had to decide between children and cousins, sharing and starvation, these were the sorry souls who didn't make the cut. The unluckiest men slept in boxes alongside the huts. One homeless man dug a hole straight into the frozen earth, building a wooden roof over this grave. These nightmare towns sprang up all around New York City that winter. On Houston Street and Broadway, five people camped out in an empty lot on the corner, using the brick wall of an adjacent building to block the wind. They insulated the walls with rags.

Newhouse wrote all of these men into *You Can't Sleep Here*, railing against the world that pushed these men to the margins. His hero stayed proud and wouldn't accept charity from his socialite girlfriend, opting to sleep in a Hooverville instead of taking shelter in her pampered world. At the climax of the novel, the homeless newspaper reporter turns down a cushy magazine job so he can stand beside the squatters in the East River camp. His decision seems self-destructive to his middle-class friends. He is beaten bloody and gassed by the cops while defending these flimsy houses.

But Newhouse backed up his story with true accounts of how the government cleared tent cities around Manhattan. In 1933, the Sanitation Department steered a red wrecking truck through a Hooverville squatter camp called "Hardluck-on-River" on the East River at ten in the morning. Flanked by fifteen workers and five cops, the city superintendent commanded the two hundred and fifty men living there to evacuate the site.

The New York Times wrote about the attack:

> . . . there was no revolt, no resistance. The men turned back into the ramshackle driftwood, tin and linoleum shacks to pack their few personal possessions. A few of the more stolid types—eleven nationalities were represented

in Hardluck—loaded their quilts and things on go-carts and headed for nowhere in particular. All morning and up to 4 o'clock in the afternoon the wreckers tore down the makeshift dwellings with the great hooks set in the rear of the red trucks. The campers sat on the edge of the pier and looked on, with a pathetic melancholy not unmixed with curiosity in the working of the juggernaut.[27]

In Newhouse's novel, however, the homeless men refuse to leave the shacks they've built, so the police descend upon the camp. They ax open a crack in the locked doors and pitch canisters of tear gas inside the houses. Newhouse's hero gets a face full of tear gas, a memory drawn from his time on picket lines, from attacks at factories, and from breadline riots:

Maybe you have been insane for one period of your life. Do you remember the moment before you went mad or didn't it happen all of a sudden? Or maybe you have had fever dreams of a particular kind. Or is it possible that your dentist may have gone insane and began drilling your eyeballs instead of your teeth?[28]

Newhouse deconstructed the world around him, rewriting his own career as he took part in historic events. But he was also part of a larger literary movement. Before the Great Depression, Mike Gold called on writers at *The New Masses* to produce a new kind of fiction, an idea he labeled "proletarian literature." In his essay, he described the range of work he hoped to include:

. . . letters from hoboes, peddlers, small town atheists, unfrocked clergymen and schoolteachers. Everyone has a great tragi-comic story to tell. Almost everyone in America feels oppressed and wants to speak out somewhere. Tell us your story. It is sure to be significant ... Let America know the heart and mind of its workers.[29]

His letter to readers spawned an entire literary movement. In *The Radical Novel in the United States*, the literary scholar Walter Rideout counted seventy such novels published between 1930 and 1939. Almost all these novels have been forgotten today, but Rideout's book counted novels by Henry Roth, Josephine Herbst, James Farrell, and Richard Wright. For a few years during the Great Depression, Newhouse's *You Can't Sleep Here* became one of the most well-known examples of the genre, though the book has been out of print ever since.

INTERLUDE
"The Irretrievable Cent of Fate"

Even though our Great Recession officially ended in 2009, many American workers will suffer the lingering effects of the economic disaster for decades to come. In 2010, the economist Till von Wachter testified before the Joint Economic Committee of the US Congress about the quantifiable and long-lasting effects of any recession, explaining that:

> The average mature worker losing a stable job at a good employer will see earnings reductions of 20% lasting over 15-20 years. While these earnings losses vary somewhat among demographic groups or industries, no group in the labor market is exempt from significant and long-lasting costs of job loss.[30]

The stories in this book remind us how these effects linger far after the recession or the Great Depression has ended. Workers wounded by an economic disaster can take almost twenty years to truly recover. Wachter outlined how these effects spread:

> A job loss is also typically followed by an extended period of instability of employment and earnings. During this period, job losers can experience declines in health. In severe downturns, these health declines can lead to significant reductions in life expectancy of 1 to 1.5 years. The

consequences of job loss are also felt by workers' children, who can suffer from the consequences even as adults, and by their families. All of these costs are likely to be greater for the long-term unemployed.[31]

The poet Delmore Schwartz graduated from college into the black heart of the Great Depression. In his short novel *The World is a Wedding*, he captured the lingering effects of economic catastrophe. Published in 1948, the book follows a group of aspiring writers, journalists, and playwrights as they stumble from the safety of the university into the grim reality of Depression-era New York City.

Even though by 1948 a decade had passed since the economic catastrophe, Schwartz spends the entire book measuring his characters' personal failures against the collapse of the American economy. "[W]e are both failures," one character declares, graduating college at a dire moment. "[W]e have to be young men in a time of failure and defeat, during the black years of the great depression."[32]

Even after the Depression ended, Schwartz's characters still struggled under the invisible pressure of diminished job expectations and compounded failures. More recently, economists have confirmed that workers graduating from college during a recession feel the aftershocks of the economic disaster for many years.

Schwartz confronted these cold realities with a lyrical sense of fatalism. During the Great Depression, he published a poem called "Tired and Unhappy You Think of Houses." In the poem, a struggling young writer imagines what it would be like to be rich and secure, fantasizing about an alternative life with a fireplace, servants, and a cozy mansion. "Tired and unhappy, you think of houses / Soft-carpeted and warm in the December evening,"[33] he wrote.

The soft vowel sounds and delicate fantasy is shattered by the roar of the subway train: "break this / Banal dream, and turn your head," Schwartz wrote, snapping us out of his own poetic daydream.

In another poem, "A Young Child and His Pregnant Mother," Schwartz captured the exact moment in a kid's life when the invisible injustice of the world first appears. The title alludes to the fact that the four-year-old hero will soon lose his status as a favored only child. He only has a vague sense of the world's awesome and dangerous power, a world which is as unfathomable as the subway machinery roaring beneath his feet.

> At four years Nature is mountainous,
>   Mysterious, and submarine. Even
> A city child knows this, hearing the subway's
>   Rumor underground. Between the grate,
> Dropping his penny, he learned out all loss,
>   The irretrievable cent of fate[34] . . .

The boy lost his treasure to the spooky underworld beneath the subway grate, and then suddenly tunes into the inherent unfairness of life. By empathizing with this image, one can catalog the minor failures, disappointments, and injustices that destroyed one's own faith in a friendly universe. In a sense, we are all perched over the void looking for a lost penny—an undefined promise that was never fulfilled.

In *The World is a Wedding*, one character described how Americans love to pretend that we have not failed; that we have not been marked by economic forces far beyond our control:

> [T]he motive of competition is made the chief motive of life, encouraged everywhere. Think of how competition is celebrated in games, in schools, in the professions, in every kind of activity. Consequently, the ideas of success and of failure are the two most important ideas in America. Yet it's obvious that most human beings are going to be failures, for such is the nature of competition.[35]

Schwartz's work can remind us of our destructive urge to hide failure. It's a dangerous trait, repressing the trauma of our economic disaster—years before many of our citizens could recover.

2. MAXWELL BODENHEIM

"Poems Exchanged for a Hamburger"

Maxwell Bodenheim sprawled against a tall green fence in Washington Square Park on May 22, 1933, watching the world begin to thaw. Rows of poems flapped above his head like halos. He wore a bright blue shirt and red tie, gaudy colors that popped in the sunlight. The next day, reporters from both *The New York Times* and *Washington Post* mocked his shirt in their pieces about him. This was precious publicity for a writer perched at the top of a long slide into obscurity.

This was the Raven Poetry Circle's first ever "Poetry Street Fair" in Washington Square Park. They tacked poems to a ten-foot-tall green wall beside a tennis court, selling them for pennies. Bodenheim was there to make some extra cash. His hair was slicked back, a flourish from his heyday in the village in the 1920s, but his black locks were thinning from age and malnutrition. The poets around him stenciled their names on the fence and organized their rhymed and metered poems into clusters.

Bodenheim's work wasn't as neat as the work of the other poets. His "Electric Song" was almost like rock and roll: "Suicide in my wires. That's my weakness now. Suicide in my wires, she's my baby now."[1] He carried the same sign all day long:

POEMS BY MAXWELL BODENHEIM
FOR 25 CENTS
AUTOGRAPH COPY 50 CENTS

Before the Great Depression, the newspapers called him "The King of the Greenwich Village Bohemians," and he published a steady stream of poetry and novels about boomtown New York. I found a photograph of Bodenheim from 1929. He was reading from his book while surrounded by eight beautiful women in evening gowns. The drunken poet grinned like he'd just won the lottery. The women draped their arms around him while he read.

Bodenheim was a true writer-celebrity, renowned during a time before television, gossip magazines, and the internet provided the fame-hungry with more alluring alternatives. Bodenheim hit his peak in a time when a writer with a steamy story could make international headlines, but his career did not survive the Great Depression and his own destructive urges.

His publisher was once Horace Liveright, the man who published *In Our Time* by Ernest Hemingway, before the young author headed to Scribner. Newspapers around the country followed Bodenheim's exploits. He was one of the first literary bad boys to run amok: women threatened suicide, ran away from home, and (in the case of one socialite) drowned themselves to get his attention. However, a few weeks before the poetry fair, Liveright's publishing house had declared bankruptcy. Bodenheim was there because he had bills to pay.

Francis Lambert McCrudden, the man who founded the Raven Poetry Circle in the early 1930s, stood under a shade tree in the park with his arms crossed. The poet perpetually scowled in his pictures, emphasizing the life of a worker and the value of toil. In his poetry, he was the complete opposite of Bodenheim.

McCrudden stripped to his shirtsleeves and vest as the day got hotter, but he never took off his white hat. Years before, he had retired from the telephone business to write poetry, but his forearms were still thick with muscle. The Great Depression suited him. He founded the Raven Poetry Circle in the early thirties with an epic poem called "The Nickel Snatcher," all about the dignity of poverty and collecting pay-phone coins. His poem "With Apologies to a Forgotten Villager" reflected the Depression-era sternness that he embraced:

> The old saw has it, "Riches prove the man."
>
> But the real test is Poverty, by damn.
>
> Am I aware the rhyme is false? I am.
>
> But even so, it tell the truth, by damn.[2]

Bodenheim didn't sell a poem all morning, even though he was the only published writer in the park.

After the stock market crashed, he floundered like everybody else, drinking heavily and struggling to find work. He took a desperate trip to Los Angeles in the mid-1930s, wheedling to get his novels turned into films. His quest failed. He wrote to his wife: "My position has become untenable here. The people with whom I'm staying can scarcely scrape their bread together, and I can't impose on them much longer."[3]

The poets milled around on the corner of Thompson and Washington Square all Sunday. They were half pan-handlers, half artists. They all needed help and they weren't in a position to bargain or turn down anything that might come their way. The poet Ruth Rappaport pasted up a lonely little sign beside her work on the fence: "Poems exchanged for a Hamburger."[4]

Bodenheim didn't know it, but his career as a published novelist was almost over. His novel *Manhattan Madness* had just flopped at bookstores. The book's hero is obsessed with money. "Christ! Everything's hard when people haven't any money," he explains on a bitter journey around Greenwich Village. "They're all set for loving but they get ill-tempered over every little thing because they're tired out and their nerves all chopped to pieces."

The poet was no stranger to poverty. In 1923, Bodenheim published *Blackguard*, a novel about a young poet living in the big city. His hero loses his job and sits in a city park, scribbling a surreal image of a great Greek poet selling fruit in a big city—wondering how writers and stories can survive in the modern metropolis: "Filled with the alert meeting of hope and bitterness he wrote with a degree of fluid ease that had never visited him before, and for the first time his lyrics grazed a phrase or two that rumored recalcitrantly of a proud story known as beauty."

After he finished his final novel, *Slow Vision*, Bodenheim spent the rest of his career as a writer cum literary vaga-bond. The Raven Poetry Circle would become his business model. The bestselling popular novelist ended up begging for support.

Slow Vision studies two lovers struggling to survive in New York City during the Great Depression. In one of my favorite passages, Bodenheim describes the same feeling that haunted me throughout 2009: "There's something wrong with this world all right, but I can't put my finger on it . . . Something must be wrong when a fellow can't get a decent wage, can't tell when he's going to be fired, can't look forward to any promise of happiness. Something is rotten somewhere."[5]

Bodenheim explores the lives of Manhattan clerks and workers, forced by managers to work longer hours for less pay. He could have been describing the way modern office workers scurried around hopelessly during our own recession. He mastered the art of describing the hunched bodies and the deadened emotions of all those traumatized by impossible choices: work kills his protagonists. But they are forced into this lifestyle; it is the only lifestyle left for them. One character quits her intense waitress job and sees five more women at the door, desperate to fill her spot.

Slow Vision also criticizes the overall reach of Roosevelt's National Recovery Act, an attempt to create fair workplace standards across American industry. His overworked waitress sees little hope in the initiative. Bodenheim wrote:

> Her lunch-room had an NRA card in the window, but its only import in her life had been a raise of two dollars a week—fifty cents deducted for cleaning the aprons—and an eight hour day stretched to nine, or ten, by devices such as a tacit hint 'to come down a little earlier, if you can,' and unpaid overtime work classified as 'voluntary service for the good of the business.'[6]

The Literature of Failure

Bodenheim's *Slow Vision* asked a question that still resonates today: why don't we read and write books about ourselves during economic collapse? He wrote:

> Why didn't they write about what was going on every-where? What was the idea? It was really true, she could walk into any bookstore and pick up ten books at random without finding a single story that dealt with people like herself and Ray, real flesh-and-blood people pouring out of the factories and offices, and the big-stores, and the booze dives, and what they went through, how they lived, how they dragged their feet back to depressing rooms like the one she was in and tried to make a dollar stretch like a six-inch rubber band, and soak their legs in hot water to take some of the ache out of them.[7]

Slow Vision failed miserably and has been swallowed by history. The book flopped upon publication and only a few copies remain, scattered and abandoned in libraries. I paid more than $50 for a copy at a rare books site—not because Bodenheim's work is highly valued, but because it is nearly extinct.

I've checked out every single Bodenheim book I could find at my local libraries. At the LAPL Central Library the checkout sleeve for his poetry collection still contains an obsolete computer punch card, the brittle cardboard only stamped once since 1930: May 15, 1981. I found more of his poetry in a rare archive of the *New Masses* magazine, whose seventy-five-year-old pages crumble when you touch them.

The book was shelved beside the works of Edward Newhouse in the proletarian novel genre. Literary scholar Walter Rideout actually looked into sales figures for radical novels: top sellers only sold around 3,000 copies, while most radical novels sold less than 1,000 copies. Mainstream publishers needed to sell at least 2,000 books before they could recoup the money spent publishing the novels. In the mid-1930s, the radical writer Henry Hart bluntly assessed the fortunes of the proletarian novel: "sales such as these mean that bourgeois publishers are going to begin to refuse to publish our novels. And, of course, they were going to refuse to publish them as the present incipient fascism increases."[8] By 1940, the genre had been effectively wiped clean from the canon.

In the first decade of the twenty-first century, the recession also pounded corporate publishers. During the darkest moments, one novel emerged at Random House that cheered the whole industry. Dan Brown had waited years to turn in his follow-up to *The Da Vinci Code*. It was almost a joke in the industry. One, two, and then five years passed since his first book became one of the bestselling novels of all time. In the spring of 2009, Dan Brown finally turned in *The Lost Symbol*. The book blew up. Brown sold a million copies in a single day. The emerging eBook market played a tremendous role in boosting these sales. Amazon slashed prices on digital books to $9.99 and made eBook delivery simple—setting an unsustainable precedent but driving a preponderance of readers to buy the eBook instead of the hardcover.

As the publishing industry stumbled and the economy collapsed, Brown preached a spacy kind of magical thinking, buffering his escapist ideas with a seemingly solid wall of facts. *The Lost Symbol* concludes with a lengthy speech by one of the main characters, who explains the great secret pursued by secret societies, wealthy men, and cold-blooded killers:

> You want a real answer? Here it is. If I hand you a violin and say you have the capability to use it to make incredible

> music, I am not lying. You do have the capability, but you'll need enormous amounts of practice to manifest it. This is no different from learning to use your mind, Robert. Well-directed thought is a learned skill. To manifest an intention requires laserlike focus, full sensory visualization, and a profound belief. We have proven this in a lab.[9]

If readers believed hard enough, they could succeed. Brown constructed his books with impeccable care, loading the top and bottom of every scene with a lecture about architecture or archeology. The characters spoke in undergraduate lecture hall monologues, every character preening like a professor. Brown's prose spoke to the bewildered masses, all of us trying to make sense of a busy and threatening universe where some were still on top and most were seeing their fortunes plunge. Nothing is more reassuring during an economic downturn than certainty: a wall of facts, an ironclad exposition giving certain dimensions and historical importance to every object. In Brown's imaginary world, characters can escape a villain's evil plan if they just believe hard enough. As the middle class imploded, Brown sold us a thriller that treated middle class values as powerful facts, creating a Potemkin village where America was still strong.

Bodenheim had no such illusions. In *Slow Vision*, his character had a decidedly bleak life philosophy that would never make the bestseller lists:

> Men, until old age, were expected to prove their worth by fighting adversities and "coming out on top," according to the message driven into her by her elders since her birth. [B]ut it was the beginning of a realization that she, Ray, and so many other people, were held down, and soured, and pushed around, by just one thing, lack of money, money, money—the great, sickening tom-tom, flesh-pulverizer,

the grinning siren always chased by millions of calloused
hands with broken, dirty fingernails . . .[10]

"Why don't people write books about things the way they
are?" begged Bodenheim's character. But he already knew the
answer: nobody wants to read about failures when everything
is going wrong and there is no hope that it will ever get better.

Birth of the Writers Union

New York City recorded its coldest day in fourteen years in
the winter of 1934. A massive snowstorm buried the city. The
city hired more than 4,300 unemployed workers to help clear
the streets. This was a ragged snow shovel army tunneling
through the drifts.

The Hudson River froze, sending up clouds of frost
smoke. Cold air vented along the chunks of ice like an Arctic
ice flow. *The New York Times* reported that a man even decided
it was too cold to kill himself. When the police showed up to
stop him from leaping to his death, he explained his decision:
"when I opened the window to jump, gentlemen, it was so
cold that I changed my mind."[11]

During the winter storm, the police explored a few of
the remaining Hooverville camps in the city. They told the
New York Times reporters that the homeless residents were
"comfortably warm."

How could anybody sleeping outdoors in a frozen city
ever be "comfortably warm?" Somebody was lying. Was the
city pretending to take care of these lost creatures? Or was
the paper trying to reassure a ragged readership about the
decency of the universe? Or did these homeless men lie about
their lives to keep their dignity?

The city counted 4,370 men and 80 women staying in city shelters during the blizzard (compared to the nearly 39,000 people in the shelter system in 2011). One man froze to death during that black night, huddled behind a building, trying to take shelter from the storm.

It would be a disastrous winter for Bodenheim. His mother died back home in Tennessee and *The Washington Post* declared *Manhattan Madness* the Worst Book of 1933.

In one of his very first poems, "Poet-Vagabond Grown Old," Bodenheim eerily anticipated his middle-age decline:

The dust of many roads has been my grey wine.

Surprised beech-trees have bowed

With me, to the plodding morning

Humming tunes frail as webs of dead perfume,

To his love in golden silks, the departed moon.

Maidens like rose-flooded statues

Have bathed me in the wine of their silence.

But now I walk on, alone.

And only after watching many evenings,

Do I dance a bit with dying wisps of moonlight,

To persuade myself that I am young.[12]

Bodenheim's brain never stopped working. A crumbling sex scene in *Slow Vision* ended with sleepy ellipses and flaccid sentences. He wrote: "Her senses also drooping, felt disappointment too indistinct to be painful and yet . . . it was hellish when you were both so tired . . . so so tired . . . you both fell back and slept."[13]

Historian Monty Noam Penkower counted 1,400 unemployed writers on the New York City relief rolls in the mid-1930s. In 1934, Bodenheim joined the newly formed

Unemployed Writers' Association, a group that quickly amassed 500 members. They held their first meeting in Irving Plaza. The group proposed a number of ways to put writers back to work, seeking a $30-a-week salary for writers working on new projects. They teamed up with the 2,000 members of the more prominent Authors League. According to Penkower, they lobbied Washington, DC for a massive writing project where 500 writers would fan out over the United States to write an "hour-by-hour account of one day in the life of a person in his community." After a few months of rejected proposals, the association evolved into an officially organized body: the Writers Union.

In the spring of 1935, Bodenheim crashed the New York City welfare office and begged for relief. Bodenheim hadn't earned a dime since his final novels flopped. He was working on a manuscript called *Clear Deep Fusion*, but he would never finish it. His visit to the relief office was his last stand. The *New York Herald Tribune* mocked Bodenheim's ragged demonstration: "he wore high shoes without laces, his shirt was dirty and the rest of his clothes needed cleaning and pressing. He was unshaven, very pale and his hair was mussed."[14]

He brought along five Writers Union activists and a squad of reporters in an effort to inspire other writers to go public with their struggles to survive. One activist waved a sign that read STARVATION STANDARDS OF HOME RELIEF MAKE REAL GHOST WRITERS.[15] Four years earlier, New York State established the Temporary Emergency Relief Administration, spearheaded by then-Governor Franklin D. Roosevelt. According to historian Monty Noam Penkower, it was "the first comprehensive relief program" in the country. Nevertheless, writers could barely scrape by on the funds that it offered.

"Writers Demand Work." The poet Maxwell Bodenheim, flanked by two fellow writers, applies for government relief funds in 1935. Photo courtesy the Library of Congress.

As the reporters watched, Bodenheim applied for relief. The government unemployment stipend would give him $14 a month for rent and $20 a month for food, about $530 a month by today's standards. His story ran in a number of newspapers the next day. Overnight, Bodenheim transformed himself into a symbol for thousands of writers who had no way to support themselves. They would join his cause, fighting for more jobs, for better working conditions, and for a fair wage for writers.

The writer Michael Sweeney has been obsessed with the life and work of Bodenheim since 1978. By his own count, he has compiled 1,500 pages of dense biographical material about the forgotten writer, including photos, signed first editions, FBI reports, an autopsy report, piles of original periodicals, essays, public talks, and recordings.

He described Bodenheim's life at the end of this dark decade:

> He was now destitute, far more than most members on the picket line. For the last 10 years he had been able to support his family by monthly royalty checks, all gone now. But even above his poverty and proletariat cause, research unequivocally shows that he was committed to continuing support of his son and wife, divorced, but continuing to as best he could.

Though Bodenheim had now signed a contract with Macaulay, he dropped them after the strike. Bodenheim signed a new contract with Carlyle House Publishers in New York.

Sweeney outlined the situation:

> In January 1935, Max applied for Home Relief and was not successful. He didn't have a home, just being evicted, and he was completely destitute. His Communist affiliations allowed him to eat but his day-to-day work for the Party so occupied his time that he couldn't seem to write.

> Carlyle House, like all publishing houses, was failing and did not offer to publish *Clear Deep Fusion*. The only thing Bodenheim could publish was his proletariat poems in the *New Masses, Daily Worker,* and the *Anvil, Partisan Review,* and Communist fliers floating around New York.

Bodenheim knew how it felt to be hungry. He refused to hide it anymore. He emerged after a forty-five-minute chat with the relief administrator. "They have treated me very well," the poet told reporters, his relief application renewed. The protestors along with him hiked down Eighteenth Street waving placards until they reached the Writers Union office. He didn't know it then, but Bodenheim was the first hungry writer to march. His headlines in the newspapers would inspire more action across the country. But he took the first painful and powerful step alone, admitting to the whole world that he needed help.

"Burning Up the Pain"

A few months later, Bodenheim collapsed in front of his friend's house in the middle of the night, dead drunk and defeated. His friend called the cops. Bodenheim spent the next few days in the detox ward in Bellevue Hospital. Once again, the burnt-out novelist was homeless. After four days, Bodenheim emerged. "Due to overwork, I took a drop too much," he told *The New York Times* as he shuffled away. At a dinner party one evening, Bodenheim grew unhinged, tilting into madness. The great playwright Ben Hecht described what happened in his memoir:

> Having emptied his tenth wineglass, he proceeded to eat it. He bit of chunks of his fragile goblet, chewed and swallowed the bits of glass as if they were the finest of desserts.

"Good God," someone said, "you'll kill yourself swallowing that glass. You're a poet, not a circus freak." "Every poet is both," Bodenheim answered aloofly. He continued to talk of poetry, and to recite some of his own latest work, holding the diners fascinated by the stream of blood and words from his mouth."[16]

In one poem about Greenwich Village dive bars in the 1930s, Bodenheim mixed jazz and poetry twenty years before the beatniks. In his most beautiful moments, his tortured syntax and convoluted rhythms eluded the constraints of verse. He wrote the ultimate "sad men" poem, converting music and pain into poetry:

> Last night I had an oboe dream—
> Whistlers in a boxcar madness bringing jazz.
> Their faces stormed in a hobo-gleam,
> Blinding all the grinding wheels and singing jazz.
> The boxcar gloried in its dirt—
> Just a hallelujah made of chanting mud.
> And one old bum opened his shirt,
> Showing wounds of music in his ranting blood.
> The hoboes sang with scorching notes
> Burning up the pain into a gale of jazz.
> While sadness poured in their shaking throats,
> Like a molten bugle in a wail of jazz.[17]

At the end of his life in the 1950s, pickled with booze in a New York City flophouse, he stayed up all night drinking with Allen Ginsberg and Jack Kerouac, making so much noise that the neighbors called the cops.

Bodenheim's poverty, politics, and wounded words cleared the way for the Beatniks. While those writers revolted against a prosperous and square America, it's easy to forget how the literary grandparents of the Beats suffered through the Great Depression.

"The box-car gloried in its dirt—Just a hallelujah made of chanting mud,"[18] Bodenheim wrote, his own legacy already shoveled underground by bad sales and the imploding publishing industry. He knew all along that he would be forgotten, but he sang from the trash heap. He sang hallelujah.

Maxwell Bodenheim once again slouched at the Raven Poetry Fair in 1936. The fair had become a faithful institution during these discouraging days, an annual bit of press for the poor writer. He had long since lost contact with his family. He depended on the spare change he earned while selling poetry. One newspaper reporter parodied the sorry group selling poetry in the park:

> Once more the sturdy fence at Washington Square South and Thompson Street bore its burden of handwritten, typed and mimeographed sheets. The occasional thud of a tennis ball on the inside of the enclosure was a disconcerting novelty, but otherwise the sound effects were merely the gay, chattery, wistful comments of poets on parade.[19]

The reporter mocked one poet for misspelling "saddest" and "pallor" in her poems. The feature ended with a sarcastic quotation of a seven-year-old poet who tried to sell poems in the park. The lines still make me sad: "Whispering shadows pass away / when the children go to play."[20] McCrudden had made a new rule for the fair, allowing poets from around the world to join provided that they subscribed to the anthology. He wrote: "send three or four plainly typed poems to your beloved editor and he will find a place for them On The Fence. There will be no charge for this gilt-edge service and if poems are sold, the purchase price will be sent to you Sans Delay and Sans Deduction."[21]

The poetry circle also unveiled the Emile Du Mond Prize for the best lyric poem of the year of sixteen lines or less. The prize totaled five dollars. Florence E. Bryant won for her poem "Earth."

The poet John Cabbage joined the poetry fair that year. He worked in the sanitation department, steering a garbage scow and writing poems. He was a minor celebrity, using the junkyard as a metaphor in the newspapers. The year before, he earned a short mention in *The New York Times*, in an article about a contest to write a song for Manhattan.

The report gently mocked the entries but noted that Cabbage had not submitted: "One great hope of the city departments ... who daily drifts to see on floating heaps of somewhat decayed asphodel as captain of a Department of Sanitation garbage scow."[22] A 1939 article about a dying Broadway play also evoked the garbage-man poet: "By chance John Cabbage might pen an appropriate ode on the riverward procession, but more probably a teamster's tender hands will ensconce the number in the ashcan."

At the fair, Cabbage wore a white-brimmed hat and smiled for the cameras. He shared McCrudden's obsessive focus on the life of the worker, exemplified in his poem about street cleaners: "He shampoos and manicures the City's streets / For he is the Barber of the Streets."[23] His work survived in the working-class margins of the publishing industry, from the Raven Poetry Fair to the Department of Sanitation's little magazine "D.S." The publication had 4,600 subscribers at the height of the Depression, selling issues for 10 cents apiece. It included poems by Cabbage, a meditation on garbage cans ("Sing a Song of Can Can"), a paycheck poem by a financial officer ("The Payrolls Must Go On"), and an anonymous boat poem ("Ode to a Scow").

Cabbage published *Tide and Time* in 1938, his final collection of verse. His book ended with a few lines to his future readers:

> I haven't any, and I won't have any
> Children—to starve and carry on the struggle
> In this world of which I am so weary,
> A world which is for the few, by the many.
>
>
> My writings are my children, my crew.
> These when I am gone I will leave to you.
> These are as I am, bitter and blue.
> From them you'll learn—at worst you will laugh; I hope
>   you will too.
> As my life keeps on I hope my writing will grow, too,
> From the man who has always felt blue,
> To the world—to you;
> To the men of the New York.[24]

Seventy years later, modern-day Ravens have many different publishing tools at their disposal. From blogs to self-publishing to digital books, anybody can publish anything. Not all self-publishing ends in desperate obscurity, either. Amanda Hocking landed a four-book deal with St. Martin's Press for her work. According to *Crain's New York Business*, Amazon bid more than $2 million for the *Watersong* series. Her series begins with a book called *Switched*, the story of a beautiful troll princess exchanged for a human baby. The troll princess grows up, unaware of her royal and magical family. As a high schooler, she falls in love with a handsome student: "He just stared, the way I stare at the TV when something boring's on. I feel compelled to look, but I don't really care or even notice what's happening."

Hocking's characters describe every emotional state in excruciating detail, a writing style seeped in the confessional mood and endless analysis of reality television.

At the same time, John Locke became the first self-published author to sell one million eBooks through Amazon. In the Wild West atmosphere of the self-publishing revolution, his novels hit some strange notes. For instance, *Lethal People* featured a wisecracking hero with some bizarre sexual banter:

> I said, "Damn, those pomegranates are amazing!"
>
> "You mean these?" she said. She ripped off her bra, and my brain circuits spun like tumblers in a slot machine.
>
> "Now, Donovan!" she said.
>
> "Now?"
>
> She stepped out of her clothes. Licked her lips.
>
> "At your cervix," I said.
>
> We made love like teenagers, wrecking the sheets, rolling all over the place.[25]

The self-publishing field evolved rapidly during the recession. Thousands and thousands of aspiring readers tried to reproduce the magic formula that Hocking and Locke established. They found themselves lost in a flood of novels, trying to figure out how to find readers in an increasingly crowded publishing landscape.

The Federal Writers Project Begins

In September 1935, Franklin Roosevelt established a federal arts program, extending WPA relief to the artists of America. The program had four divisions: music, drama, art, and literature. The president gave the new outfit $27 million for a projected six-month project. The writing arm—the Federal Writers Project—had some modest goals: to produce a five-volume guidebook series about the United States, to create "an encyclopedia of government functions," and "to record the unfolding legacy of the WPA."

Bodenheim was one of the first writers hired for the new project. He wrote about different corners of the city, taking the opportunity to explore his own past. In one essay for the project, he described his path from the Midwest to New York City as an epochal exodus. He wrote:

> A second change of a different nature began in Greenwich Village shortly before 1910. It had a slow, quiet beginning, scarcely perceptible to the neighborhood itself; yet it was to make that dingy backwater celebrated wherever the English language is spoken. At that period materialism had assumed an unprecedented importance in American life. Ambition not directed toward the goal of a large bank account was almost alien to thought and education, and, like most things alien, was regarded with distrust and scorn. Above all was this attitude adopted toward the struggling artist seeking satisfaction from completion of a poem or picture. A natural result was the withdrawal of the rebel artist into protective groups. Many of these groups gravitated to the larger cities Kansas City to St. Louis, St. Louis to Chicago and finally, from all over the country to the metropolis.[26]

As the program grew, the supervisors decided to let a few select employees, including Bodenheim, work from home so that they could focus on personal work. The experience nearly ruined Bodenheim's recovery. As soon as Bodenheim left the structured confines of the project, his drinking spiraled out of control.

Former FWP supervisor Jerre Mangione remembered the novelist's weekly office visits: "He would arrive at the building in a semi-inebriated state; then, unable to summon enough will power to enter, would go to a bar across the street and continue his drinking. Eventually, it would take two of his project friends to escort him, protesting and staggering, from the bar to the office." Early in Bodenheim's career, the critic Louis Untermeyer described how the poet's alcoholism and chronic failure blended into his poetry:

> Bodenheim has something that [none] of his colleagues . . . possess. I refer to his extreme sensitivity to words. Words, under his hands, have unexpected growths; placid nouns and sober adjectives bear fantastic fruit. It is a strange and often magic potion he brews from them; dark and fiery liquids that he pours into curiously designed cups. Sometimes he gets drunk with his own distillation, and reels between preciosity and incoherence. Sometimes the mixture is so strong that even his metaphors, crowding about each other, become inextricably mixed. But as a rule, Bodenheim is as clear-headed as he is colorful. Among the younger men he has no superior in his use of the verbal nuance.[27]

Bodenheim remained separated from his family through most of the Great Depression. His son Solbert even made a complete break with his father. He had once been a poetry celebrity, running with T. S. Eliot, Ezra Pound, and Conrad Aiken. He cheated on his wife but mailed letters whenever they were apart. They were two bright young poets stranded in reality.

Maxwell Bodenheim got divorced in 1938 and promptly
married a woman named Grace Fawcett Finan. She died of
cancer in 1950. Bodenheim helped care for her as she struggled with the disease. The loss broke Bodenheim. His biographer found him pouring ketchup and water into soup for
food. He married Ruth Fagan in 1950, a troubled younger
woman. Biographer Jack B. Moore described the decrepit
poet's final years:

> Bodenheim stumbled corpse-eyed again through his
> old haunts, shuffling slack-limbed like a caricature from
> Hogarth's "Gin Lane." He wrote poetry still and sold
> some for drinks, and he received handouts from old
> friends such as Louis Cohen, who operated a laundry on
> West Eleventh Street. Bodenheim always tried to supply
> poems to repay friends, and Cohen cherished his collec-
> tion of unpublished Bodenheim manuscripts.[28]

In 1954, Bodenheim was murdered in a Manhattan flophouse
with Fagan, killed by a deranged drifter in love with her.

***

Way back in 1918, Maxwell Bodenheim wrote a love poem for
his ex-wife, Minna, opening with one of his trademark metaphors. Bodenheim's crazy style seems almost archaic now:
his high-wire act doesn't feel quite as revolutionary anymore:

> The wrinkled grimaces of eastern skies
> Are caught on the Chinese mirrors of your eyes
> And lie, pallid and benign.
> Your mouth is a senile dragon
> Spitting fire-fly words from its vermillion shroud.[29]

The poem captured the earliest stages of a romance: he loves
her, but he can't say why; nevertheless, he tries over and over

to explain. His lines get tangled up inside each other. These poems live on, strangely enough, through free poetry sites on the internet. These sites copy love poetry from out-of-copyright books and reframe them as stand-alone love poems.

We should remember how Bodenheim blazed like a disintegrating rocket ship for a few mad years, rather than focusing on the dark and empty place where he crashed.

INTERLUDE
"A Kind of New Normal"

In "A Letter to Eileen Myles," the contemporary poet Susan Briante sketches out her family finances in a few stark lines, sharing the debt and meager earnings of a poetry professor in a new sort of economic confessional poetry. She teaches poetry at the University of Texas at Dallas. She writes:

> What do you make of our economic avant-garde? We work in state institutions; we work for private colleges, we work in offices with views to air conditioning equipment on roofs . . . Farid and I have $15,000 in savings, $40,000 in debt. In 40 years we've seen privatizations, a loss of price cautions, a rise in sun block.[30]

This blunt poetry fascinated me. In an email exchange, Briante explained how the Great Recession steered her poetry in new directions:

> In a poem such as "A Letter to Eileen Myles," I talked very directly about my husband's and my decision to have a child and how economics played a part in that decision . . . I think it's important to share this information in poems and in conversation as we try to come to an understanding of the effects of the new economy.

How can you bring children into the world while trying to survive in a wrecked profession? Briante channeled her family anxieties, her miscarriage, and the birth of her daughter into five years of powerful poetry. Her work is a revelation.

Out of all the literary occupations, poetry is the least lucrative. The same financial problems affect all writers, but poets feel it most acutely: they practice a craft that fewer and fewer people understand. Our culture no longer values the vocabulary and skills needed to appreciate their challenging art form. No effective system of patronage exists to protect them. Briante's poems ache with a dilemma nobody ever discusses, problems that can swallow a family whole: "Farid and I do not have time, do not have wealthy parents, no Girl Scout skills."

Wealthy parents have subsidized generations of writers, but the poetry world is dominated by increasingly expensive MFA programs and a dwindling number of grants. Poets should not have to choose between children and writing. Poetry should not only belong to wealthy writers who can manage the lifestyle. "There is a potential for devastating effects on our community that might be hard to perceive," said Briante. "How do we gauge the art that isn't made because someone can't carve out the time to write the poem?"

Her poetry confronts the effects of grinding poverty and our casual acceptance of this new economic reality: "I worry about the insidiousness of the current economic crisis— stagnant wages, increased costs (for health care, housing, and education), limited job possibilities, etc.—which can hardly be described as crisis but has become a kind of new normal."

Briante experienced this sense of urgency as a poet and as a family member. Both of her brothers were unemployed when I interviewed her in 2013. She teaches poetry to a generation that will enter the workforce with record levels of unemployment and debt. "My household income puts me squarely in the middle class," she said, "but I feel more and more vulnerable despite my increased earnings. The slope to financial security has become a lot steeper than it once was. When you come from the working class (as both myself and my husband do), you don't have a safety net."

Briante grew up in New Jersey. She spent a year living in the city. When asked about her time in New York, she replied: "I don't necessarily feel I was part of any New York poetry scenes—of which there are many—but I was exposed to so much poetry and art. I still find it very revitalizing to visit. I also learned a lot from people about how to create and sustain an artistic practice. That lesson was invaluable to me."

Her recession-era work grapples with our economic woes in a way directly inspired by the sad men and women of the Great Depression. Her collection *Utopia Minus* opens with a poem that personifies the stock market as a "fumbling baby boomer." The poem begins: "The Market migrates; the Market scatters across the Metroplex. The Market dreams my carcass onto the highway . . . "[31]

"I wrote the poem at the dawn of the financial crisis," she explained to me.

> At the time, I was really dismayed at how the stock market seemed to be the only indicator of our economic health that the news media and policy makers were talking about. And the reporting on it was always personified: the Market reacts, worries, stumbles . . . etc. I took the

subjects out of the first few lines of the poem and replaced them with "The Market" in the poem's second stanza.

To her students, Briante cannot promise meaningful solutions or hope for a more fulfilling writing life. Instead she teaches them about a lifestyle of compromises:

> I talk to my students about how they might create a life that will allow them to make art beyond their undergraduate or graduate degrees. I also talk to my students about the kinds of 'marketable' skills they learn in a poetry workshop (or any lit course): the ability to understand and analyze complex texts, the ability to make use of and offer respectful critique, etc. I know some of my colleagues find it crass and apologetic, but I think it is elitist to imagine our students have the privilege of enjoying our classes without worries about their prospects in the workplace.

These problems should clutter all of our literary discussions. Writers should obsess over these contradictions. We need to find new ways to make these issues visible again across all disciplines. Writers of the 1930s stirred up a rowdy street war, forcing newspapers to pay attention. No writer should flounder alone. I hope we are remembered as a generation that made noise as we drowned.

3. ORRICK JOHNS

The One-Legged Poet

When he was seven years old, Orrick Johns jumped the trolley tracks in Saint Louis, ducking between streetcars as he played tag with his friends. He leapt across the tracks in one of those stupid and brave moves that kids make, trying to bridge some impossible gulf. He didn't make it. The train car shredded his leg to the bone. They rushed him home and called a surgeon. Johns nearly bled to death while waiting for the surgeon to arrive. His father held his hand while the doctor sawed off his leg on the kitchen table.

Johns recalled the incident in his memoir: "As I lay in bed I was acutely sensible of a great loss. It seemed to me that the world and my brothers were growing way beyond me; and that I would never catch up. I recall a pang of envy when they came back in the Spring full of the story of winter sports."[1] Perhaps the crippling loss prepared him for the Great Depression, robbing him of any romantic illusions about idyllic childhood. Childhood for Johns meant sacrifice and the surgeon's hacksaw.

When the Depression hit, Johns was working as a handyman. He then landed a $10-a-week job with the Communist party on the West Coast, hired to coordinate worker strikes around the country. During one California strike, he helped ranch hands fight to earn a living wage. After the six strike leaders were arrested, a masked mob of forty men broke into the jail and kidnapped the leaders. In the desert, they whipped the leaders with tug straps, clipping their heads with sheep clippers and smearing them with red enamel. When the bloody workers crawled back into town, the local doctors refused to take care of them.

The one-legged poet did not flinch from the brutal realities of the labor struggle. In 1933, he traveled to New York City just in time to witness the chaos of the Great Depression firsthand. Johns visited a Hooverville homeless encampment that stretched for an entire mile along the banks of the Mississippi. In St. Louis, Johns found countless vagrants living on houseboats and shacks beside the river. Policemen would beat them if they tried to enter the city, so these exiled citizens survived on whatever they could fish. He discovered an entire community of unemployed men living inside massive concrete pipes abandoned at a shuttered construction firm. "There had been something ship shape and self-respecting about those pipe dwellers,"[2] he wrote.

Amid all the squalor and violence of 1933, Johns witnessed a new fighting spirit emerging in America. He described the feeling: "in the solidarity which unites even a small band of loyal and serious people, threatened by violence, there is great strength. Unlearned then that the more helpless half of mankind is, after all, of a collective habit, and cannot live without that feeling of cooperation for self-defense."[3]

Orrick Johns's first marriage ended in 1932. He was living in Carmel, California with his wife Caroline and their two-year-old daughter, Charis. Johns edited a local newspaper there and the family stayed at Caroline's mother's house. His wife suffered from an undiagnosed mental problem, "a condition in which a thousand thoughts and impulses crowded the brain at once; and her only recourse was to remain perfectly still, obey none of the impulses, but let them pass in a dizzy array."[4]

At the supper table, his wife would freeze with her fork perched in space. She would repeat the ritual over and over again for an hour before eating. During a morning swim on one chilly morning, his wife swam deep into the ocean to try to drown herself in front of her family. Johns wrote: "The beach was absolutely deserted except for myself and the kid playing in the sand, and every now and then running too close to the water. My anxious excitement communicated itself to the child, and when I picked [Charis] up, her silent, troubled look seemed to indicate that she knew what was happening too."[5]

Johns was helpless along the beach, unable to swim, unable to understand his wife's condition. His wrecked country had little protection for the fragile lives of the mentally ill or handicapped.

Miraculously, the police rescued Caroline and she was institutionalized. Johns left his daughter with his mother-in-law. He later reprinted one of his wife's poems from this period in his memoir:

Oh God,
Slow down these wheels!
Make me the arc of a larger circle;
Deepen my beat.[6]

Reflecting on these troubled years, the poet Kenneth Rexroth wrote a sentimental tribute to Dylan Thomas and the poetry scene that they shared, begging the dead poet to explain what happened to their dead friends. "They are murdering all the young men," he wrote, calling out to a generation of poets. The poem wonders: "[what became of] Orrick Johns / hopping into the surf on his / one leg?"[7]

Soon after arriving in New York City, Johns started freelancing for the *New Masses*. They quickly promoted Johns to poetry editor. Johns recalled these days in his memoir:

> It was a very different New York, the aspect of it that I saw. Gone the Bohemianism and cynicism, the concern with sex and aesthetics that I remembered. Most of the people I knew had been hit hard by the depression. They were beginning to see that their professional lives depended on some form of organization. They were joining artists unions and writers' unions, picketing in strikes of publishers and newspapers, and even walking in the ranks of department store workers. There was a solidarity among office workers and shop workers and professionals which would never have been dreamed before.[8]

By his own estimate, Johns read 400 poems every month for the magazine. In the mid-1930s, the *New Masses* averaged about one poem a week. That spring of 1934, Maxwell Bodenheim stumbled into the offices of the *New Masses* with a new poem called "Revolutionary Girl."

New Masses editor Joseph North described the hobo poet: "Bodenheim came through that doorway, his blond hair up, unruly, a cowlick in the back, a smell of alcohol like an aura about him, and was converted to the cause of the proletariat. He compared the two worlds: the affluent where he had been; and the disinherited where he now was."[9] Bodenheim wrote a poem with strange images of Russia, imagining a better world where everything was not crumbling to pieces:

And in the Russia of today

   Men and women, proud of working-hours,

Sturdy, far from blood-steeped tinsel,

Take their summer vacations

On the steppes, in cleaner games,

   In flowers, pledges, loyalties,

Clear-growing, inevitable,

Deepening in their youth.[10]

Johns had spent the 1920s running around Greenwich Village with Bodenheim, two promising poets competing in the prime of their lives. Bodenheim wrote strange and tangled poems, but Johns had a more lyrical reputation. Bodenheim dominated the spotlight during their early days, and eventually Johns stopped writing poetry altogether. The declining literary rock star even wrote a poem dedicated to Johns:

O tangled and half-strangled child, you shrink

Forever from yourself, and wear a pose

Of nimble and impenetrable pride.[11]

Bodenheim saw the bottled rage of a child cheated out of his childhood in Johns and predicted the shimmering potential that would drive Johns to become a powerful leader during the Great Depression. Bodenheim described his old friend in a poem:

Yet sometimes, wavering on the sudden brink

Of jaded bitterness, you drop your clothes

And weave a prayer into your naked stride.[12]

Relief

Johns lost his job at the *New Masses* in the summer of 1935, but he promptly received the most important assignment of his entire life—a directorship at the newly formed Federal Writers Project in New York City. The program aimed at replacing the mind-numbing jobs facing the literary trade with new projects.

Johns managed to channel his impulses into solidarity and administration. the *New Masses* would stay afloat as other paying outlets evaporated. It published poetry by countless writers, including Richard Wright, Kenneth Fearing, and Bodenheim himself. Johns spent the rest of the Depression heroically resurrecting the careers of hundreds of writers, skillfully managing the resources of the Federal Writers Project. This one-legged poet would carry his friends through the catastrophe of the 1930s.

Headquartered in the enormous Works Progress Administration building at the Port Authority, the FWP opened in October. This bureaucratic beehive paid more than 600 writers around $20 a week (about $300 today) to collect information, write guidebooks, and record folk histories, among other projects. Nationwide, the FWP would employ around 6,600 writers at its peak.

Johns was tasked with picking writers from New York City's demoralized talent pool. He wrote in his memoir: "They were all from the home relief rolls, and it took weeks for some of them to get the habit of clean shirts and pressed trousers. They ran the gamut of mental states, the scared and the stolid, the humble and proud, reserved and excitable, with a scattering of plain drunks."[13]

When Johns first arrived, the Port Authority office was a mess. Johns and his deputies sent writers scavenging in trash bins for boxes to use as desks while they waited for chairs.

The only thing they didn't have was a shortage of unemployed workers looking for help. Even when supplies started to roll in, chaos ensued. A simple order for pencils got crisscrossed on somebody's supply list and the New York office ended up with mountains and mountains of writing utensils stored in crates. The FWP just kept them, rather than fill out more paperwork. His supervisors sent workers home with hundreds of pencils apiece.

The Novelist Anzia Yezierska described the first jubilant payday in her memoir: "men who hadn't had a job for years fondled five and ten dollar bills with the tenderness of farmers rejoicing over a new crop of grain."[14] A young novelist named Richard Wright particularly caught her eye: "his well-modeled head on straight built shoulders stood out among the white faced men drained by defeat."[15] Wright told her that in his Chicago neighborhood people were singing "Mr. Roosevelt, you're my man" as the New Deal took effect in the mid-1930s.

***

What would a twenty-first-century Federal Writers Project look like?

In 2008, the journalist Mark I. Pinsky wrote an essay for *The New Republic* calling for a new federal writer's project to save thousands of journalists from losing their jobs while print media crumbled. Pinsky had lost his job as a religion writer at the *Orlando Sentinel* in a humiliating round of layoffs. As internet prophets urged writers to embrace the chaotic economy of the web, Pinsky argued that a fundamental economic shift had occurred. He dared to state the truth: writers needed help.

Millions of Americans keep detailed records of their lives on Facebook pages, on their Twitter feeds, and in other online networks. In some way, everybody is a writer now. But we have fractured our national narrative into self-absorbed and ultimately incomprehensible fragments. Perhaps the job of the next writer's project could be to curate this awe-inspiring mass of content, helping the country tell itself stories again. A new Federal Writers Project could work to make our digital legacy comprehensible for future readers; to both preserve our ephemeral online stories and to create a more cohesive narratives from the vast online repositories.

Pinsky offered these suggestions for putting out-of-work newspaper reporters back to work:

> . . . the FWP could begin by documenting the ground-level impact of the Great Recession; chronicling the transition to a green economy; or capturing the experiences of the thousands of immigrants who are changing the American complexion. Like the original FWP, the new version would focus in particular on those segments of society largely ignored by commercial and even public media. At the same time, the multimedia fruits of this research would be open-sourced to all media, as well as to academics. As an example, oral history as a discipline has made great strides in the past 70 years, and with the development of video techniques, the forum of the Internet could make these multi-media interviews widely available to schools and scholars, as well as to average Americans.[16]

Most of the people responded to the article with scathing criticism. One anonymous reader wrote: "I didn't see him writing years ago to save the 8 track tape or dot matrix printers, and print media is equally as outdated. I hate to see people lose jobs, but that is life sometimes, and government is not a panacea."

A reader named Jeff was particularly blunt:

> Go and develop new skills that are in demand in the marketplace and get yourselves another job! The government already supports "artists" who can't create a painting or sculpture that another person actually wants to buy. What a stupid thing that is and it should be stopped immediately. You don't have any kind of "right" to a job in journalism and any kind of "right" to be paid to write a single word. Tough luck. Either get another job, or go live in your parents' basement and start a blog where you can complain all day and night about how you can't get a job writing.

I felt a swell of hope reading Pinsky's essay in 2008. I could imagine President Obama setting up some new program. I could imagine a sturdy, tough, but powerful solution to our problems. I dreamed about working for the twenty-first-century WPA. The article no longer remains online, but it once stood as a monument to the wrath of amateur internet pundits and the blistering scorn waiting for anybody who suggests a bailout for anyone other than bankers. Even Pinsky's peers knew it wouldn't work. He told me in an email: "Other journalists found it intriguing, with zero chance of happening. A few right wing media cranks reacted predictably."

We could never rally around clear economic interests. George W. Bush had left a legacy of unrestricted finance and military spending. We inherited a deregulated financial universe and nobody could build a WPA on that framework. The revolution never arrived in 2008. We limped away like wounded animals, suffering quietly in our caves.

Pinsky blamed middle-class writers for this defeatism:

> . . . in the 1930s journalists considered themselves a part
> of the working class, largely identified with the political
> left, and understood the power of collective action. In
> the post-Watergate era, journalists became white collar,
> college-educated, and middle class, often upper-middle
> class. They disdained collective action, and saw them-
> selves as above politics and ideology. And so, they were
> unable to slow, and thus cushion, the inevitable decline
> of newspapers.

I, like many of my fellow writers, was part of this trend. We
emerged from relatively privileged backgrounds and earned
advanced degrees in writing. I studied English literature at
the University of Michigan and my journalism career began
with a New York University master's degree. Several generations of journalists before me had entered the profession from
high-powered universities. Even though most of our salaries
placed us closer to the working class, it took many years for
twenty-first-century journalists to fight for unions.

Poetry and literary writing are no different. While MFA
programs and journalism schools have provided a living wage
for many writers, they also raise the educational bar, driving
kids to take on more loans. If writers have not identified with
workers since Nixon, then we hardly have any hope of saving
ourselves again with any sort of labor organization. The irony
is that even though most of my peers have entered the profession from high-class places, we will never earn enough to join
the upper middle class. Someday soon, the only remaining
"working" writers could be people who can afford to support
themselves through grants, other work, or an inheritance.
Pinsky has grown more pessimistic since the grim winter of
2008: "Unlike the 1930s, when the economy improves, living

wage jobs in journalism are not coming back anytime soon, if ever."

"The Turmoil of the Present"

During my months working in New York University's Bobst Library, I found a dusty copy of *The New York City Guide*, a seventy-year-old book packed with maps, etchings, and strange stories about New York City. Johns was the first supervisor of the sprawling Federal Writers Project, leading one hundred and fifty writers as they collected material to include in the book. The guidebook opens with a sweeping stream-of-consciousness tour of Manhattan, a movie montage love poem for the city:

> The morning sun picks out an apartment house, a cigar store, streams through the dusty windows of a loft. The racket swells with the light. These shoes are killing me, she said, taking the cover off the typewriter. Main Central is up to forty-six. Did you read about the earthquake? Looms, shears, jackhammers, trolley cars, voices, add to the din. And in the quieter streets the hawker with the pushcart moves slowly by. Badabadabada O Gee! Hawkers of vegetables, plants, fruit. Badabadabada O Gee! In half a million rooming-house rooms the call penetrates ill-fitting windows. The boy who came to be a writer is waked in his mid-town room and dresses for his shift on the elevator.[17]

In 1936, things looked grim for the unfinished project. Franklin Roosevelt was gearing up for a rough election season as winter thawed, and the first critics of the Federal Writers Project emerged. Johns marshaled his scrappy but unfocused crew of writers to justify and protect the work they were doing.

During a period of clear-minded stability, Maxwell Bodenheim produced a magnificent essay about Greenwich Village. The essay paid homage to his glory days in the Village before World War I, when the Village was the birthplace of the bohemian movement: "In Greenwich Village the earliest rebels found comparative quiet, winding streets, houses with a flavor of the Old World, and cheap rents." He described the often candlelit meetings of Village intellectuals:

> They talked of their work, of the arts, or of sex and Freud; and were secretly thrilled at doing so in mixed company. They discussed Socialism, the I.W.W., woman's suffrage, and the philistinism of the folks back home. The conversation ranged from brilliant to silly, but always, instinctively or consciously, it was unconventional. And throughout, they drank endless glasses of tea for these were the days before Prohibition and bath-tub gin.[18]

One hundred and fifty writers had been toiling on the guidebook for months, but they had made little headway. As critics grumbled, the government sacked Samuel McCoy, the FWP supervisor above Johns, citing "insubordination and inefficiency."

McCoy didn't go quietly. In the papers, he blamed left-wing conspiracies. *The New York Times* reported: "he said most of the employees were members of the writers' union and the city project council and that they had been devoting most of their time and energy to factional activities against nonmembers."[19]

Other employees said the project was 90 percent populated by Communists and left-wingers. *The New York Times* didn't bother to check the facts. Johns struggled to keep control of his writers and resources during this poisonous period.

But politics were certainly not the only problem. Nobody had quite figured out what these writers were supposed to do. They had been hired to write a guidebook about the city, to dig through archives, to research everything from zoos to shop girl strikes, to survey New Yorkers, to record city folklore, to do a thousand conflicting and impossible jobs.

Former FWP supervisor Jerre Mangione described these troubled years at the WPA: "They were psychologically incapable of planning for the future. Caught in the turmoil of the present, they lived from day to day in constant dread of losing their jobs and in mortal fear of the growing Nazi menace in Europe."[20] The "turmoil of the present" combined the crippling anxiety of economic downturns with a nagging sense of future dread and real-time worries. These are the feelings that keep workers trapped at dead-end jobs, that stop young families from buying houses, that stall efforts to unionize during turbulent times.

Despite his best efforts, even a simple pamphlet that Johns published about New York State could not satisfy Washington, D.C. His supervisor chastised the poet for including lurid details about the city, copy "afflicted with the cheapest sort of ballyhoo . . . . Lurid intimations of Chinatown dens, the come-on stuff of the tourist barkers." The pamphlet generated scathing editorials in conservative newspapers around the city. The WPA was forced to issue an official apology in 1937.

On August 22, 1936, the WPA fired three hundred New York City employees in a single swipe. The shocked workers refused to leave the WPA offices, mingling with another group of activists who were marching for better relief payments for the unemployed. The relief protestors carried around an empty baby-sized coffin, memorializing the three-year-old New Jersey boy who starved to death after his family was dropped from the relief rolls. DON'T LET THIS HAPPEN IN NEW YORK, read their signs.

As the protests boiled over at WPA buildings around the city, Raven Poetry Circle member Marie Margaret Winthrop, who was also the secretary of the American Writers Association, hand-delivered an angry letter to Orrick Johns. The Association accused the FWP administrators of favoring Communists. They were specifically upset that Johns had hired a *Daily Worker* reporter to serve as his publicity officer.

I have a picture of Winthrop from the Raven Poetry Circle archives. Her hair is brushed back and the May sunshine illuminates her features. She has high cheekbones and a simple smile. She lounges against a park fence with the casual demur of a catalog model. She wears a long skirt, a leather jacket, and a white blouse with two or three buttons open. She clutches her notebook in one hand.

In her poem "White Roses," she writes:

I've gone mad with the clatter of falling bric a brac
Mad with the clash of wheels within wheels

The din of falling god is a tinny sound
Like the sickly color of pink
The sharp staccato shrillness of idols falling
And the falling of a million men, are the little sounds
Almost drowned by the noises of the rushing years.
But I can hear them--

All the overtones and undertones

Of an insane symphony.[21]

With her crazy imagery, her loose line, and her leather jacket, she anticipates the Beatniks as she describes the apocalypse. She has the most rhythm of all the Ravens. She channels the pop pop pop of new wave poetry, wiggling out of the tight constraints of formal verse.

In 1936, the director of the National Youth Administration outlined the size of the Crisis Generation in a *New York Times* essay, recording some grim statistics about American workers between sixteen- and twenty-four years old:

> . . . more than one in seven are heads or members of relief families. Of the 600,000 who live in urban areas and are of school age, 300,000 are not in school and are not working or seeking work. Considerably more than half have had work experience, but three fourths of these are unskilled or semi-skilled, and only five percent of the whole unemployed group of young people consists of skilled workers.[22]

In October, thirty-five unemployed writers showed up at Johns's office to mount a hunger strike. They were more members of the American Writers Union who were struggling to be heard. Though the country seemed to be recovering from the Depression, they wanted to remind the world that many writers could not find work. They decided to sit and wait without eating until jobs were forthcoming.

Johns didn't call the police. He let the demonstrators sit in his office during the whole futile hunger strike. There were no more jobs coming, but these demonstrations made headlines for days. The unemployed writers traded chairs with FWP writers throughout the workday. They were peaceful, but they set a powerful precedent. These writers would not wait for work or slink off into the shadows. However, the hunger strike only lasted all of twenty-six hours.

On account of the bad publicity, the WPA caved to their demands and granted Johns the ability to hire fifty more workers. They also began wondering about his control of the situation. Back in Washington, other officials planned ways to kick the one-legged poet out. Nevertheless, these protests marked a turning point. On the surface, the country seemed to be recovering, but these protests made the truth of the situation very visible—making front-page headlines for several months straight.

Scorched-Earth Bookselling

Something happened during the Great Recession, something we seldom discuss as writers, as workers, or as citizens. We stumbled out of that dark time with a completely consolidated economy. We now live in a world ruled by monopoly, where everything from mayonnaise to airlines to publishing is in the control of a very small group of powerful companies. In January 2017, a young legal scholar named Lina M. Khan diagnosed our new condition in a paper in *The Yale Law Journal* called "Amazon's Antitrust Paradox." In 2019, I covered one of her keynote speeches at the PubWest conference in Santa Fe, New Mexico where her radical ideas about monopoly enforcement produced a long standing ovation from a roomful of booksellers.

The legal scholar described a "monopoly crisis" in the United States that arose after a fundamental shift in antitrust enforcement in the 1980s. "More than any other firm, Amazon depicts how a company can come to monopolize all sorts of markets without triggering scrutiny under our anti-monopoly laws," Khan said, detailing the online retailer's "sheer dominance" of the publishing marketplace. "Amazon is seller of books, a publisher of books, a printer of books, and dominant in both the e-reader and e-book markets. It is both a third party marketplace and a merchant of its own private labels, creating a huge conflict of interest," she said. This unregulated landscape enabled the rise of our present corporate oligarchy, a government run by a clown who takes credit for a stock market that only enriches the wealthiest citizens and siphons resources straight from his working-class base.

We saw the powerful effects of monopoly when Borders declared bankruptcy in February 2011. Within days, 200 stores were shuttered. The company briefly entertained hopes of a buyout bid or auction, but these deals also collapsed and so the company tumbled into liquidation. Borders Group President Mike Edwards posted his unhappy resignation: "We were all working hard towards a different outcome, but the headwinds we have been facing for quite some time, including the rapidly changing book industry, eReader revolution, and turbulent economy, have brought us to where we are now."[23]

Box stores like Borders changed the literary economy drastically, pushing the market toward consolidation and monopoly. Borders built a bookselling juggernaut in the mid-1990s by creating a revolutionary computer inventory system that could track a book's popularity through changes in stock around the country. Bookselling moved from relying on human choices to computer-generated sales. Editor Paul

Constant explained the transition in a brilliant essay about working on the Borders sales floor:

> Our displays were bought and paid for by publishers; where we used to present books that we loved and wanted to champion, now mediocre crap was piled on every flat surface. The front of the store, with all the kitchen magnets and board games and junk you don't need took over large chunks of the expansive magazine and local-interest sections. Orders came from the corporate headquarters in Ann Arbor every Sunday to change out the displays. One time I had to take down some of the store's most exciting up-and-coming fiction titles (including a newly published book that was gathering word-of-mouth buzz, thanks to our booksellers, called Harry Potter and the Sorcerer's Stone) to put up a wall of Clash CDs. One month, for some reason, the cafe sold Ernest Hemingway–branded chai.[24]

In the 2000s, the department-store mentality was triumphant. There was no union to protect Borders employees. There was nobody to stand up and fight as these jobs evaporated. When Borders closed for good in September 2011, the remaining 399 stores and 10,700 employees were out on their own.

Any dissent was stranded in online discussion boards and quick blog posts. Thousands of readers shared pictures of signs that read WE DON'T HAVE A BATHROOM, TRY AMAZON inside the closing stores. Gallows humor took the place of real anger. The debate was quickly framed in two ways in the media: either a badly managed corporation had collapsed or else the eBook revolution had taken its first major victim. Our headlines focused on bookselling trends instead of on a floundering workforce at the mercy of brutal capitalist necessity.

Both these narratives excluded the fates, futures, and feelings of thousands of workers. Massive numbers of the newly jobless swamped the unemployment rolls in September. Nobody—from the publishing industry to the local government to federal arts societies—offered any official support for these unemployed workers. We failed our first major test as a collective literary community in this new recession. We never made national headlines fighting to replace or maintain these jobs. None of us were staging hunger strikes at Borders. The publisher and bookseller Dennis Johnson described on the *MobyLives* blog the new ecosystem:

> Publishers are on a crash course learning how to survive without any volume booksellers, and in an environment with one retailer (oh, guess) representing as much of its business as—well, who knows? Eighty percent? More? That alone is likely to make publishers give up on printing books—there's no sense in printing books if your main outlet isn't going to order any until they sell them—and join the digital 'revolution.' In short, B&N's scorched earth policy of the 1990s has ultimately left us with, well, scorched earth. If the book is going to survive it, it's going to take some real revolutionary activity, indeed.[25]

If Johnson's prophecy comes true, big publishers will have no resources to support fledgling authors. Conglomerate publishers will continue to shave margins, pushing more midlist writers into the indie publishing scene. Writers' collectives could ease the workload and streamline marketing. These writers could form stronger bands in this post-apocalyptic landscape. The landscape will be crowded with stranded writers: sooty survivors will have to band together to survive.

***

Johns started drinking heavily and avoiding his job altogether as the protests continued. He cursed the mounting paperwork on his desk, a rainbow of "white, salmon, blue, pink, yellow and green" documents that he had to present to Washington every day. He kept a brave face for *The New York Times*, boasting that the guidebook project had produced an epic manuscript: "The total volume to date, more than 8,000,000 words, dwarfs the combined wordage of the three 'jumbo' novels of the day . . . plus all of Shakespeare and the King James version of the Bible."

His deputy Travis Hoke struggled to keep control of the office in Johns's functional absence, but the job only aggravated Hoke's own emotional instability and drinking problem. As work spiraled out of control, Johns stumbled into an all-night party in October. At some point during the historic bender, a red-headed sailor cornered the drunken poet. The sailor drenched him with booze and lit the poet on fire. "When I woke up, some of my teeth were scattered on the floor and blue flames were rising around my face,"[26] he wrote in his memoir.

Party hostess Doria Jordan beat out the fire and took him to the hospital. It was 8:55 in the morning when Johns arrived at the hospital, just as dawn was breaking in the chilly October morning. The police reported fractured ribs, lacerations of the face, burns on both arms, lacerations of the nose, and the loss of two upper teeth. The one-legged writer had spent his whole life editing poets; he was never meant to fight. It took Johns weeks to recover. He resigned from the FWP in December, dogged by scandal over the incident at the party and his work as a Communist. Johns would never publish poetry again.

He married his third wife and fled to Connecticut, drinking his way through writing a memoir. Johns ends his memoir by explaining why he quit the Communist party for good, mainly because the work became "increasingly dry dull and repetitious." His fellow Communists focused on the minute political details of everyday decisions, whereas Johns preferred to be "outside the party and able to enjoy Brahms symphony No 1 in c minor without his comrades critiquing the decision."

The New York Times reported his 1946 suicide: "drinking a poison concoction he mixed in a glass of beer."[27] At the end of his memoir, Johns writes a curious passage:

> . . . if I have a final confession to make about the family, it is that we Johnses have often regarded ourselves as idealists—and idealists are often self-deceivers, (as the reader may have discovered from this book). My worst enemy I think has been the habit of self-deception and it always catches up with you in the end. Sooner or later you find out that you have been fooled by your own mind.[28]

He never outright lists these self-deceptions, but he talks about his break from the Communists and his slave-owning grandfather. Partly thanks to his ignoble end, Johns's life and legacy has been scrubbed from the literary record, but maybe there is still some idealism left worth sifting out from among the ashes.

INTERLUDE
Sad Men

"We will have so much winning if I get elected that you may get bored with winning," Donald Trump crowed early in his presidential campaign, stoking our twenty-first-century appetites for success. For more than a century, writers, politicians, and popular culture have maintained the illusion that success is available to anyone in America, even when upward mobility has been destroyed by obvious economic realities.

Early in the twentieth century, Andrew Carnegie hired a young journalist named Napoleon Hill to interview successful men and distill their "secrets of success." Carnegie had decided that Americans spent too much time in school. In his opinion, half of our education "had no value whatsoever in connection with the business of earning a living or accumulating riches." Hill claimed that he studied the lives of 25,000 people, finally publishing the book *Think and Grow Rich* in 1937. Publishers have sold 70 million copies of the book since the Depression. His book boils down to one single idea: "before we can accumulate riches in great abundance, we must magnetize our minds with intense DESIRE for riches, that we must become money conscious until the DESIRE for money drives us to create definite plans for acquiring it."[29]

In the wreckage of the Great Depression, Hill constructed the myth that personal desire trumps class, poverty, and economics. He taught a new generation to tune themselves to the powerful music of money, pushing the idea that merely believing that you will be rich can actually make you rich—unwinding all the ideals that WPA workers fought for every single day. While workers around the country organized to earn basic liberties, Hill celebrated individualism and capitalism without constraints. He mocked unionization as some kind of cheat:

> Millions of men and women throughout the nation are still engaged in this popular pastime of trying to GET without GIVING. Some of them are lined up with labor unions, where they demand SHORTER HOURS AND MORE PAY! Others do not take the trouble to work at all. THEY DEMAND GOVERNMENT RELIEF AND ARE GETTING IT . . . if you are one of those who believe in trading their votes to politicians in return for the passing of laws which permit the raiding of the public treasury, you may rest securely on your belief, with certain knowledge that no one will disturb you, because THIS IS A FREE COUNTRY WHERE EVERY MAN MAY THINK AS HE PLEASES, where nearly everybody can live with but little effort, where many may live well without doing any work whatsoever.[30]

The Depression wasn't the fault of the stock market crash or mass unemployment: Hill blamed our weak, selfish minds. "Focus on accumulating wealth" says Hill over and over again, a bad magician distracting us from the difficult and tangled history of the Great Depression, repackaging the novelist Horatio Alger's rags-to-riches stories as self-help science. Hill's legacy has persisted, from self-help books to political campaigns to our enduring literary canon.

Melanie Stefan, a lecturer at the School of Biomedical Sciences at the University of Edinburgh, diagnosed how this obsessive focus on success hurts science in a column for *Nature*. She wrote: "As scientists, we construct a narrative of success that renders our setbacks invisible both to ourselves and to others. Often, other scientists' careers seem to be a constant, streamlined series of triumphs. Therefore, whenever we experience an individual failure, we feel alone and dejected."[31] To counterbalance this false "narrative of success," she proposed that scientists create an alternative "CV of Failures" to rest alongside our normal CVs filled with all the times we have succeeded. We need to stop pretending that failure is un-American. We all fail, over and over, during the course of our working lives.

One of the most popular cultural artifacts of this recession period was the AMC drama *Mad Men*, which follows the decadent lifestyles of New York City advertising executives in the early 1960s. The show explored the suburban landscapes chronicled in books by John Updike and John Cheever, the middle-class scribes who wiped the 1930s off the literary map. The fortunes of these "Mad Men" rise and fall as a result of their ability to help themselves, to take control of their own American destiny.

In contrast, the writers in my book are "sad men." We have systematically scrubbed the stories of these sad men and women who wrote during this radical period from our English classes. We don't want to remember the booze-soaked failures, the doomed hunger strikes, or the literary Communists. We want a workforce and a literature that succeeds by willpower and individualism alone.

4. ANCA VRBOVSKA

In downtown New York City, a Czechoslovakian immigrant named Anca Vrbovska struggled to make a living during the Great Depression. She was unhappily married to a baker and spent all her free time turning her misery into working-class verse. She wore her poverty like a badge in the poem "Comfort":

> Comfort smothers the spirit and changes
> A slender snow-white swan
> Into an indolent, fat goose . . .
> Comfort must be shunned like pestilence
> By those who aspire to live,
> To fight, to fly, to sing.[1]

I found her picture in a stack of Raven Poetry Circle photographs at the New York Historical Museum. She has high cheekbones and a big grin. She is one of the only poets who stares straight at the camera. She likes to wear vivid prints: brilliant checkered dresses and patterned blouses. Her mop of curly hair explodes in all directions, as if her brain is cooking from too many poems.

Vrbovska lived two blocks from Sheridan Square, the center of the Bohemian universe. During the early 1930s, her neighborhood was a center for both writers and out-of-towners: anybody drawn to wild parties during Prohibition. Bohemians like Vrbovska were treated like tourist attractions. The *New York City Guide* from the 1930s described her neighborhood:

> This is the focal point for tourist night life in Greenwich Village; revelers from the Bronx, Brooklyn, and Queens arrive, as evening approaches, on the IRT subway, by bus, taxi, and private car to visit night clubs and bars that abound in the square itself, line West Fourth Street to Washington Square, and dot the neighborhood north and west. This, too, is a center for Villagers who frequent more modest establishments—unpretentious saloons, lunch wagons, and cafeterias. A cafeteria, curiously enough, is one of the few obviously Bohemian spots in the Village, and evenings the more conventional occupy tables in one section of the room and watch the 'show' of the eccentrics on the other side.[2]

Vrbovska was trying to write books at the worst moment for publishing in the twentieth century. According to *Publishers Weekly*, the total number of books produced between 1929 and 1931 dropped from nearly 211 million to 154 million. In a speech to the Massachusetts Library, Little, Brown & Company publisher Herbert F. Jenkins confessed that sales were down 25 to 33 percent in 1932. He advised publishers to continue this massive reduction of book production for their own survival, recommending a 30 percent decrease in production for 1934 and then 40 percent the next year. In one of her poems, Vrbovska twisted a nursery rhyme into a surreal poem about fate, religion, and money.

The dream is a cradle
Rocked by Death's slowest hand.
Swing me, swing me,
Gently sing me
For the angels soon to ring me
Into God's cash register.
In his palm—what a coin,—
Where will he toss me?[3]

As one of the Great Depression's coldest winters loomed, Vrbovska obsessed over the creeping chill. She writes a poem called "Autumn Wind," describing leaves tumbling off the trees: "they abandon themselves to the cruel destructive love of the wind."[4]

Her poem was the first one printed in the first Raven Poetry Anthology. Today we would call it a zine: four sheets of paper stapled together. Individual issues cost a dime; a yearly subscription went for a full dollar, accompanied by a red faux-velvet cardboard binder to hold the year's run. The first issue of The Raven Poetry Circle Anthology hit the streets in December, containing poems by Francis McCrudden, Ruth Rappaport, and Vincent Beltrone.

In one issue, McCrudden attacked the journalists that mocked his club in the summer. His editor's note mixes the self-published authority of zines with the self-righteous tone of the early blogosphere:

> Some of the critical cuckoos and alleged wits of the Village have been doing some hooting of late, and it pleased them to great the first number of our modest and unassuming little Anthology with catcalls, Bronx-cheers, and other unseemly noises . . . knowing well that the raucous animadversions of the bozos referred to will, in all

probability, do us more good than harm, we are somewhat pleased; without intending it, they have done us a friendly turn, and we hasten to thank them for their timely condemnations.[5]

Vrbovska fled a disintegrating situation in Europe to end up in this busted America. Here, she lived alongside some of the richest people on earth, but to her the massive skyscrapers were tombstones towering over a dying city. The Anthology contains Vrbovska's poem "Skyscraper":

Giant question marks are the Skyscrapers,
In dumb amazement they stare at the sky
As if trying to guess the reason why
Puny men should build so high?[6]

Occupy Wall Street

The first Occupy Wall Street protestors set up camp in Zuccotti Park in lower Manhattan in September of 2011, creating a protest hub in the middle of the skyscraper canyons that Vrbovska once described. Over the next month, the Occupy protestors would be pepper sprayed, clubbed, and herded through orange netting as they marched around the city, sadistically humiliated by the media and the government in their quest for economic justice. On CNN, Erin Burnett smirked through a segment called "What does Occupy Wall Street stand for?", while *The Wall Street Journal* sneered at the "half-naked demonstrators, the ranting anti-Semites, Kanye West or anyone else who has helped make Occupy Wall Street a target for easy ridicule."[7] Even Todd Gitlin, in a more even-handed and sympathetic op-ed for *The New York Times*, wrote that "[t]he Zuccotti Park core doesn't seem to have a plan, or even to take kindly to the idea of consolidating a list of demands."[8]

"What does Occupy Wall Street stand for?" An unidentified speaker, photographed by David Shankbone, at an Occupy Wall Street protest in September 2011. Photo courtesy Wikimedia Commons.

The demonstrations of the thirties were exactly the same. They were restless and unending, evolving as different groups found overlapping purposes. Authors marched alongside department store workers. Poets helped farmers organize their inchoate demands.

The Occupy Wall Street activists built a makeshift library in Zuccotti Park. They published a virtual card catalog for the library online, boasting 390 books. As readers around the world explored the list, donations poured in and the collection swelled to 8,000 titles in a few months. The books ranged from the *Harry Potter* series to *The Shock Doctrine: The Rise of Disaster Capitalism* by Naomi Klein.

In 1997, the San Francisco Library pulped 250,000 forgotten books to make room for computers and reading spaces, consigning works by authors like Bodenheim to oblivion. A group of rogue librarians bucked these orders, stashing books in safe nooks and stamping them with imaginary checkouts to keep them in circulation. They called it "guerrilla librarianship." *The Atlantic Monthly* defined the term as "the use of surreptitious measures by librarians determined to resist the large-scale 'deaccessioning' of rarely used books . . . [It] can also involve such tactics as transferring endangered books from one department to another and hiding books in lockers, to be reintroduced to the collection."[9]

The OWS librarians drafted a brief manifesto that updated guerrilla librarianship for the twenty-first century. "Guerrilla libraries are constantly shifting, growing, being remade, and transforming. Each day that a guerrilla library is opened it takes on a new form as new materials arrive, new labels are created for new subjects, and different librarians cycle in and out."[10]

Following the success of the Occupy Wall Street Library in New York City, Occupy libraries sprouted up everywhere. The library website even linked to occupation libraries in Spain. I visited the Occupy Los Angeles library and found a row of ragged paperbacks. In Occupy San Francisco, there was a cardboard box with a couple books inside. These were communal spaces where activists and visitors could mingle, and new books arrived every week.

During the Great Depression, the Raven Poetry Circle Anthology became a new home for struggling readers and writers: sharing news, travel plans, subscriber growth, and dispatches about the poetry fair. When Vrbovska published her first book of poems, McCrudden wrote a sprawling blurb for the eighty-page book: "Cyclone is quite out of the ordinary, bewildering whirlwinds of thoughts on life that lift one to the stars, that enable one to see this restless planet and it's still more restless inhabitants as none but the poets and demigods ever see them."[11]

Metaphors are scattered throughout the blurb like a car crash: mixing dust storms, interplanetary travel, Heaven, and our restless planet. Much of the Raven Poetry Circle's self-published prose seems corrupted by catastrophe. Their rickety, ramshackle passages seem perched at the edge of the abyss. Had the Great Depression itself infected their writing? We have no idea how it felt to read those words at the time, to identify with a writer lost in the same kind of fog.

The second annual Raven Poetry Circle poetry fair in Washington Square Park lasted an entire week. *The New York Times* returned to cover the event. The reporter mocked one poet's misspelled "Self-Portrait" and pointed out "a noticeable aversion to the use of capital letters."[12]

Despite the insults, proud poets tacked up newspaper clippings from the year before, turning press accounts that mocked them into proof of their artistic authority.

On Sunday afternoon, a storm nearly ruined the freshly typed poems. Raindrops "pelted the fence at Washington Square South with truly poetic cadence,"[13] wrote a *Times* reporter. When the rain died down, the poets encountered a tack shortage while jockeying for fence space.

Nevertheless, sales were brisk. The day's jackpot was a $1.50 sale by a poet named John Rose Gildea. According to Ross Wetzsteon's critical history, *Republic of Dreams: Greenwich Village: The American Bohemia, 1910–1960*, Gildea cut a dramatic figure: "Long-haired and wild-faced, he often wore a red leather outfit and a black hat, sported a diamond nose ring, and hung a tire chain around his neck with a glass door knob attached."[14] That year he wrote:

Good Morning God!
Good Morning Mary!
I hope Thee mought
Be bright and cheerie.
So may Ye gaze upon me kindlie
That through my days
I walk not blindlie.

Even Joe Gould—the homeless author working on *An Oral History of Our Time*, a legendary manuscript that supposedly filled thousands of pages—showed up for the fair in 1934. He wore khaki pants and a purple jacket, and his beard was thick and tangled. He had a habit of disrupting Raven meetings by squawking like a seagull. Gould published one poem in the anthology as well: "In the winter, I'm a Buddhist; in the summer, I'm a nudist!"[15] read his couplet. Many years later, the journalist Joseph Mitchell would immortalize the homeless poet in two famous *New Yorker* profiles and the book *Joe Gould's Secret*, all while trying to track down the author's fabled manuscript.

The weeklong fair captivated an eighteen-year-old journalism student named Louise Krist with its bohemian splendor. She met a dashing older writer there named Prince Childe de Rohan d'Harcourt, a Village character with a gold-topped cane and a penchant for space cadet poetry who wooed her with his favorite topic, his unpublished novel titled *Ro Dran and the Year 90,000*: "It is an erotic story of love. It is greater in its imaginative quality than the Arabian Nights. It is the most fantastic, most imaginative, most swiftly moving, most romantic story ever written."[16] D'Harcourt believed, like generations of frustrated writers before and after, that a novel could save him.

Bohemian Rhapsody

Vrbovska threw a Raven Poetry Circle party one hot night in June—a reading that changed a band of self-published poets into the biggest literary celebrities in the country. Thirty poets showed up for the party, drinking a jug of California wine and reading poetry. According to *The New York Times*, Krist arrived wearing a "grey-blue suit" with a trench-coat belted around her movie-star waist. She soon snuggled up beside an uninvited guest: her boyfriend of less than two weeks, Prince d'Harcourt.

A *Los Angeles Times* reporter took great pains to describe d'Harcourt's signature look: "He wore a pinstriped brown

suit, a soft blue broadcloth shirt, highly polished shoes with
spats and an upturned mustache with an angle of 90 degrees
at the extreme edges. His cane and pearl grey hat were in the
modes."[17] The poet had, on different occasions, claimed to be
a French prince, an Italian viscount, and an Austrian duke.
He stood three inches shorter than Louise, but had the cha-
risma of a cult leader.

Watching Krist and d'Harcourt flirt at the party, Vincent
Beltrone, one of the founding members of the Ravens, grew
jealous. Around one in the morning, he tried to pick a fight
with the dandy. Dwarfed by the six-foot Beltrone, d'Harcourt
left the party with his young girlfriend at his side. Beltrone
followed the couple for thirty blocks, trying to convince Krist
to abandon her prince. It made for a surreal scene on the
empty street: a wispy girl, a scrawny fop, and an angry poet
zigzagging across Manhattan.

"I boarded the train and I came home," Beltrone told the
police the next day. "That is the last I saw of them."[18] Louise
never came home that night, and her disappearance made
national headlines. Reporters grilled the individual Ravens
for clues, which is how these obscure poets finally made it
into the spotlight. Within days, the Department of Justice
dispatched agents to track down the girl. As the federal manhunt expanded, journalists breathlessly reported the "prince's"
rap sheet. He had flourished as a criminal in the permissive
cultural playground of the Village, breaking into houses and
running extortion schemes under a range of aliases: Gustav
Von Donwitz, Fred London, and Rohan Donwitz.

He had been arrested for grand larceny in 1914, for
burglary in 1917, for extortion in 1918, and for beating his

ex-wife in 1924. The police and journalists swarmed around Vrbovska's apartment after Krist disappeared. The teenage poet's father was a world-renowned violinist and was able to command the police commissioner's attention.

The Bohemian charm of Vrbovska's community faded in the cold light of day. *The New York City Guide* described the crooked neighborhood: "though a blaze of light by night, is, by day, an uninteresting hodgepodge of buildings of varying sizes and ages, suggesting little of the charm that lies beyond its limits."[19] The cops grilled garbage-man poet John Cabbage. Beltrone was forced to tell his story over and over again. Nobody knew what had happened to the young couple after they disappeared into the subway. The police papered the neighborhood, pasting handbills with Krist's picture on every available surface.

Two full weeks passed, but the couple had utterly vanished.

An unblemished photograph of the Raven Poetry Circle is stored at the New York Historical Museum. Anca Vrbovska grins in the middle, surrounded by the rest of the poets. All the names of the Ravens are carefully printed along the border of the photo. Beneath one young woman's image there is a conspicuously empty spot where a name should be. It is Krist. She's standing in between McCrudden and Beltrone. She smiles mysteriously.

The police questioned Vrbovska and kept prowling her neighborhood with their handbills, but the nationwide manhunt for Krist and the Prince ended on June 19, 1934, when a restaurant owner spotted the badly disguised lovers strolling down Third Avenue.

Krist and her prince had spent two weeks sneaking between Village flophouses and friends' couches, somehow eluding the police, the feds, and the press. The police were called, and the fugitive poets made a feeble attempt to disguise their identities as Mr. and Mrs. Robert White. They were promptly arrested.

Reporters swooped down on the police station that same day, and the couple demonstrated a knack for another twenty-first-century art: celebrity publicity. In a series of lengthy speeches to the press, d'Harcourt explained that "they had discovered their love would not permit them to remain separated." He immediately begged reporters for two dollars so the penniless couple could get married. Then Krist spoke: "I love him, but we're penniless. We didn't even have breakfast today. But we intend to get married and then we'll work so we can take a trip to the Orient and Russia."

Encouraged by the attention, d'Harcourt launched into a surreal statement: "I am the super-conscious mind," he intoned, waving his golden cane before a crowd of reporters frantically recording his speech. "All the forces of the universe command we come successfully out of the troublous moments and that we be married today."[20] But the marriage was not to be. The poet prince was charged with "seduction" and Krist was arraigned for being a "wayward minor." The *New York Tribune* printed the most dramatic coverage of the event, running a two-column photo of the unrepentant Bohemians staring into the camera.

When Krist's parents arrived at the police station, her father yelled: "What is the matter with you? Are you crazy? You are making a fool out of yourself!" The *Tribune* captured the priceless teenaged drama that followed: "Miss Krist's only answer was to give a defiant toss of her head, turn her back more squarely on her parents."[21] The next day a magistrate dismissed the seduction charge leveled against d'Harcourt, when Krist "emphatically" explained to the judge that she was in love. After the court appearance, one thousand people thronged outside the courthouse, vying for a glimpse of the "prince."

The arrest sent shockwaves through the Ravens. In the September issue of the Anthology, McCrudden wrote a poem entitled: "Last Word on a Recent Well-Known Incident," concluding the bizarre case in his signature style: "The 'prince' who kissed and wooed La Krist, / Was never on the Ravens' list."[22] Beltrone, his pride still smarting from the humiliating night at the poetry party, penned a vicious poem for the October issue entitled "Perspective Villagers":

> Dance until the bottoms of your feet
> Become armored,
> And in the vortex of the dance, rub your sloping breasts
> On the heaving bosom of your valiant knight.
>
> . . .
>
> Early in the morning, go home,
> Repeat to your girl-friends the experiences
> You have had in the Village.
> Tell them all about the many posing artists—
> You have met.
> But do not forget to emblazon your illustration
> With the vernacular
> "Gee and O Boy!"[23]

The scandal ended quietly. The authorities detained d'Harcourt at Ellis Island for a few weeks, hoping to get him deported. Once they discovered that the fraudulent prince was really born in Oklahoma, they released him.

Krist wasn't so lucky. While awaiting trial, she was sent to the Florence Crittenton Home. Founded by a wealthy philanthropist after his daughter died of scarlet fever, the shelter housed "lost and fallen" women. In August, a magistrate put Krist on probation with a draconian set of stipulations: she couldn't marry for two years without her parents' express permission, she couldn't communicate with d'Harcourt for six months, and she had to perform community service. That was the last mention of the case in the national press. In August 1935, Krist would publish a poem in the Anthology entitled "Mood in Ebony," perhaps describing her first days in the park with d'Harcourt:

> His love was like cocaine
> That crept into her blood
> And fed upon the substance of her veins.[24]

Letters From Europe

Vrbovska kept a low profile inside the Raven Poetry Circle during 1935. She only published two poems the whole year. "Winds and Clouds" is a restless, cosmic poem longing for some unidentified lover or muse to carry her away: "I, too, shall swiftly, endlessly race / As thoughts now race across my brain / or bursting comets across the space."[25] Later that year, she published "Vacation Reverie," once again longing for "companions whose mind / will comprehend the things I love and know":

The only time I feel a clasping hand
When I too, condescend to tread
Banalities deceptive, swampy land.
Gayly the frogs are croaking, the crows cawing,
But such advancing is more like sinking
Than upward flying, forward going.[26]

In May 1935, a *Washington Post* reporter wrote an essay about the third annual poetry fair. He was fascinated by Margaret Egri, a poet who signed her work AM 67. She said that her poetry was really composed by "Etheric Agent 975," a poet living in eighteenth-century England who was channeling verse to her through time and space. Her poetry had an appropriately mystical bent:

The grandest line may prove but memory's host
A path that leads some dreary, tattered ghost . . .
One great with glamorous form and passion's livid power
Her but the humble pilgrim trapped in this tragic hour.[27]

Bodenheim also showed up at the Raven Poetry Fair that spring, enjoying one of the last few places where people treated him like a celebrity. He wrote a poem for one of the Raven regulars, Florence Wiltshire. Another poet wrote a poem about the aging Bodenheim.

The *Washington Post* reporter was the only journalist to capture the bohemian dignity of the club: "Don't forget that Edna St. Vincent Millay was once a full-fledged Village poet, fully half as crazy as the Ravens are. And look at her now—the clearest singing voice we have."[28] That reporter counted thirty poets selling on the fence that year.

Margaret Winthrop was there too. The *New York Times*, reporter called her "an exceptionally well-dressed poet." She showed off a self-published manuscript and wore a pink shirt, blue tie, and matching handkerchief. She worked alongside the Prince D'Harcourt, now released from jail and "sedate in brown, with a long cigarette holder and a gold knobbed walking stick." He attacked the wall with his manuscript, filling up ten entire fence boards with excerpts from his science fiction masterpiece.

At the end of 1935, McCrudden published a list of his subscribers—his small magazine's proudest moment:

> Nor is the appreciation now voiced for the Raven Poets confined to the narrow limits of the Village. It is widely evidenced throughout the country, in Ohio, Illinois, Michigan, Connecticut, New Jersey, Maryland, Florida, and California, and the poets of this little group can justly take pleasure in the thought that their poetry is also known and loved beyond the rolling seas in England, France, Germany, Italy, Africa, and New Zealand. But enough. A new and we hope still a better year is beckoning.[29]

***

Soon, Vrbovska began to receive letters from home about Hitler's tightening grip in Europe. His imperial armies were growing, but the American government wasn't helping. 100,000 people marched through Washington Square Park to protest the Nazi regime's treatment of Jews. In retaliation, Hitler burned thousands of books written by Jews, stoking giant fires around Germany and preparing his ovens. Vrbovska wrote about the stars blinking out in her poem "Impression."

> They vanished as a last trembling tear
> From the weary eyelids of an unwanted child
> Who instead of a fond motherly kiss

Was lulled to sleep by his silent cries

...

His innocent dreams already darkened

By distrust and deed for doubtful tomorrows[30]

In December 1936, she wrote "The Proud White Rose" about a girl who passed out with a bottle of gin.

Now it is still night, blind buildings

Stare with their glassy eye at the sky;

In the falling snow the melody of an inaudible

Evocation for eternal enchantment trembles.[31]

May Swenson in the Village

In 1938, a young WPA worker named May Swenson showed up at Anca Vrbovska's door to interview the Raven poet for the Federal Writers Project's folklore unit. Swenson chronicled the experiences of Macy's shop girls, pharmacists, and department store union organizers, capturing their lives in detailed monologues for the FWP.

Vrbovska told Swenson a gory folktale that she heard while shucking corn with her relatives as a child in Czechoslovakia. A woman cheats on her husband with a series of three local priests, hiding them in her oven when her husband comes home to check on her. The priests hold a comical dialogue as they are each added to the oven, stuffed inside like a clown car. Her husband finally returns home for dinner, and the priests never get a chance to escape. The seemingly hapless husband mutters "Now I'm going to kill you," and the story takes a brutal turn:

And he did so. And then he pushed her in the oven too.

And then brought in kindling wood and made a big fire

in the oven, and all the four of them were burned, and nothing remained of them but their skeletons. So the poor peasant had four skeletons in his house and he didn't know how to get rid of them. And he was very worried. And naturally in the village all the churches suspended services, because there were no priests and none of the villagers knew what became of their priests.[32]

But the story doesn't end there. The murderous husband meets a clueless soldier and tells him an elaborate ghost story—tricking him into disposing of the bones at the same time. Along the way, the spooked soldier murders another priest, bringing the total of dead clergy to four.

Swenson recorded her immediate impression of Anca Vrbovska in her notes: "Small stature. Neat, compact figure. Dark hair. Dark penetrating eyes . . . Has a very expressive way of emphasizing action in her speech. Clear, deep, dynamic voice. Perhaps worth recording."[33] Vrbovska also chronicled her impression of Swenson in her diary that night: "slender and blonde, with a very pale face, blue eyes, calm, almost cold appearance . . . Shy of speech . . . Ambitious, contentious . . . Her humor is dry, cutting, subtle."

This was the beginning of a literary connection that would only grow. Swenson had stumbled into New York City in 1935 as a fresh-faced college kid from Utah, completely unprepared for the economic meltdown. She was barely scraping by until she joined the FWP, and she undertook her work with care and diligence. Though it took her many years to find her voice as a writer, she would grow up to be one of the most important poets of her generation.

Within weeks of the FWP interview, Swenson decided to move in with Vrbovska. Swenson's biographer and companion

R. R. Knudson would later publish a photo from that time that captured a visit to Coney Island: the two poets pose in front of a mural of the ocean, pretending to be perched on an ocean liner bound for some happier place. Vrbovska leans forward with a mischievous grin while Swenson leans back, one leg drawn up to protect herself while wearing a shy and sweet smile.

In her FWP reports, Swenson often archived the ephemera of department store workers, such as newsletters, in-store postings, union organizing speeches, and scraps of drugstore jingles. During one visit to a five and dime on Fourteenth Street Swenson interviewed a worker named Sue. She recorded a scrappy poem by the union organizer:

> Sure they take us out on parties,
> When we win our bonus monies;
> . . .
> We must work hard to win it,
> But it should go in our pay;
> . . .
> So sign up with the union
> For what we win is ours
> And we wouldn't have to listen to
> The bosses hearts and flowers.[34]

She also captured oral histories of strikes. One activist described camping out in Grand Department Stores for eleven days during an occupation:

> Arrangements had been made for food and bedding to be brought in, and the workers notified their families by phone that they would be away from home indefinitely. We had cots brought in and blankets, electric burners

"What we win is ours." Photographer Russell Lee gave us a brief glimpse of an unidentified woman marching in a 1936 picket line. Photo courtesy the Library of Congress.

for coffee, and plenty of eats. Although there was food and other things we might have used in the store, none of our people touched any sort of merchandise during the strike. Two engagements were announced during the time we sat in, and we held parties. We even held a marriage ceremony there for a couple who decided to get married during the strike. The girls dressed up the bride, and the fellows groomed the groom, and we had a priest sent for, and married them.[35]

During this same period, Vrbovska took Swenson to Raven Poetry circle parties in the Village and Swenson published some of her first poems in the Raven Anthology. Her poems were constantly rejected elsewhere throughout the late 1930s and 1940s. But Vrbovska wouldn't let her stop.

Swenson eventually wrote nine poetry collections in her lifetime, occasionally revisiting her old Manhattan haunts. She contemplates a department store in her poem, "A Fixture": "Women women women women / in a department store . . . between two glass revolving doors / sluff sluff sluff sluff / (rubber bottoms of whirling doors) / flick flick click click."[36]

At the height of World War II, Vrbovska received a bleak missive about her family, according to Knudson's biography: "Dear Anca, Thy sister and her family and at last thy mother were deported. They never gave us a sign about themselves and they didn't come back. Thy mother was killed in a gas chamber. Alas! I cannot write anything cheerful."[37]

Vrbovska channeled her suffering into a poem called "Good Lord":

The family gone up as smoke
Through the chimneys of Auschwitz

Good people they were
They believed IN HIM
Especially, the mother.
Her last letter--a Credo:
The good lord will not forget us
The good lord will not forsake us.[38]

Swenson spent part of the Forties as a manuscript reader at New Directions. She gave the great editor James Laughlin a copy of Anca's manuscript. "Anca's not half the writer you are," said Laughlin. Vrbovska wrote herself a different kind of ending in her poem, "Sanguine Sea":

Unafraid, exultant, and unafraid,
For the journey we have prepared
Our numb hands, inter-eager, in carnal fear,
Though motionless, cling to the Now,
Clasp the Here, with stubborn fingers,
Our unfitted hands clasp the Now, clasp the Here,
Though exultant and unafraid, unafraid,
For the journey we have prepared.[39]

Swenson's career climaxed with a $130,000 MacArthur Foundation fellowship. Her lyrical, depoliticized poems would be celebrated in the second half of the twentieth century. Anthologies would prefer this new kind of poetry, and politics would be forgotten. Swenson died in 1989 at seventy-six years old.

While Vrbovska didn't achieve the same level of fame as Swenson, she also worked as a writer and editor until her death in 1989. She published three books of poetry, long since out of print. She edited *The New Orlando Poetry Anthology*, shepherding new generations of American poets. In an interview with the Contemporary Authors series, she recalled these difficult days during the Great Depression:

> Some of our greatest American artists, poets, and writers were saved from starvation by WPA: Richard Wright, Zero Mostel, Orson Welles, May Swenson, and myself, to mention a few . . . We need a constructive art revival that not only reflects the destructive aspects of the atomic and other scientific inventions, but also its vast potential for improving life for humanity, plus outer-space explorations men of courage always envisioned . . . nations are not remembered because of their wars, but like ancient Greece, because of their artists, playwrights, poets, philosophers, and discoverers.[40]

INTERLUDE
"You Walked Right into Our Laboratory"

The gin-loving sportswriter Heywood Broun transformed the newspaper business with a single column in the *New York World Telegram*. Broun ended his August 1933 "It Seems to Me" opinion column with a promise to support a union for writers. "There should be one," he concluded. "I am going to do the best I can to help in getting one up." Even Broun's friends couldn't say for sure what he intended to accomplish with his vague offer "to help," but his column quickly spread across the entire country.

The union movement then was still confined to factories, to service workers, and to other blue-collar professions, even though many believed that labor could never mature unless it was embraced by white-collar workers like journalists. "Show me two white collar workers on a picket line . . . and I'll organize the entire working class,"[41] said Samuel Gompers, who helped found the influential American Federation of Labor in 1886 and served as president of that labor organization for nearly forty years.

In *A Union of Individuals: The Formation of the American Newspaper Guild, 1933–1936*, Historian Daniel J. Leab wrote: "By the dozens, from Boston to Honolulu, they wrote to [Broun] outlining the newspaperman's depressed economic situation in their areas."[42] Broun started hosting meetings with like-minded writers and editors at his Manhattan home. Within two months, he cobbled together a hundred and fifty newspaper workers (a fraction of the thousand "working newspaper men and women of this city," by a *New York Times* estimate) for the launch of the fledgling "Newspaper Guild of New York." This organization began with a loose constitution and three demands: a five-day, forty-hour work-week, a minimum scale for wages, and ample notice before a firing.

Under Broun's guidance, the Newspaper Guild of New York elbowed its way into public consciousness in 1934, with a series of dramatic conflicts with publishers around the city. The guild staged its first actions at the *Long Island Daily Press*, a paper recently purchased by a young businessman named S. I. "Sam" Newhouse.

Newhouse made the ideal first opponent for the guild. He was a stubborn media mogul who built his empire from scratch. Born to European immigrants in a Lower East Side tenement building, Newhouse dropped out of school in eighth grade and began a career in business to take care of his family. As a sixteen-year-old office manager, Newhouse demonstrated a nearly supernatural ability to transform failing newspapers.

As a teenager, he turned around New Jersey's *Bayonne Times*; at twenty-seven, he bought a controlling stake in the *Staten Island Advance*. He did not look fondly on organizing efforts at the papers he worked hard to rehabilitate. When forty employees of the *Daily Press* tried to join the Newspaper Guild in 1934, the paper's leadership fired eight of the union organizers.

In response, guild members spilled into the streets of Queens, where the newspaper was printed. The protesters passed out flyers about the *Daily Press* firings to businesspeople and theatergoers one evening in July. When the police showed up to stop the protest, Broun steered his congregation straight toward the police station. Despite a stern warning from the police sergeant, the picketers continued to hand out flyers while sound trucks and vehicles plastered with pro-guild posters cruised the block. The Guild amplified its outreach with radio testimonials and newspaper coverage. An airplane covered with pro-guild messages made repeated flybys.

The public spectacle never produced an official strike at the *Daily Press*. Within days of the first protests, Mayor Fiorello La Guardia brokered a peace treaty in his office between Newhouse and the guild. Newspaper employees were permitted to organize, and the Guild agreed not to hold Long Island newspapers to the same wage standards as larger New York City papers. Mayor La Guardia became a prominent supporter of the Newspaper Guild of New York during its first two years. In 1935, addressing a crowd of three thousand supporters at a black-tie fundraiser for unemployed Guild members, he quipped, "Although newspaper people are supposed to be very temperamental, they have shown that they know how to work together."[43]

These early protests were pure improvisation, an experiment staged to test both protest tactics and public response to the action. Leab described the aftermath of the highly publicized picket: "Newhouse, who could not understand why the guildsmen had singled out his newspaper, told Broun: 'you've made a guinea pig of the Press.' [Broun] replied: 'Well, you walked right into our laboratory.'"[44]

It didn't take long to drag Newhouse back into Broun's social experiment. Later in that summer of 1934, the Guild defended the reporters and staff at the *Staten Island Advance*—the suburban paper that laid the foundation for Newhouse's entire newspaper empire—when the mogul fired an editorial writer and Guild organizer for his "incompetence."

The protest began with an enormous gathering. A thousand supporters rallied in the middle of Staten Island's business section. To rile up the crowd, Guild members steered a sound truck through the streets, broadcasting boycott messages through loudspeakers. One of the organizers bragged that "in the last twenty-four hours, the head of almost every labor union on Staten Island has promised his support." The New York Typographical Union was the first blue-collar union to back up his claim. The major printer's union brought moral support, but also brought workers to swell the threadbare ranks of the newspaper reporters and editorial workers on the picket lines.

One week later, Newhouse returned to New York after a European vacation with his wife. Heywood Broun and his guild picketers met the cruise ship at the harbor with loudspeakers and a protest boat. This was a public relations masterstroke that inspired more New York City newspaper headlines. Soon, the guild even picketed outside the mogul's home in Manhattan, bringing the suburban battle into the

city. "I will not be intimidated by picketing, hippodromiz-
ing, or ballyhooing,"[45] Newhouse told *The New York Times*,
comparing protesters to the gamblers who fixed horse races,
which is what he meant when he invoked the long-forgotten
art of "hippodroming."

The protests ultimately produced no legal repercussions,
and the fired employee was never reinstated. The picket lines
gradually faded out and the rival newspaper fizzled after a
week of production. Worst of all, the *Staten Island Advance*
circulation actually increased during the picketing, a humiliating problem for the Guild that was trumpeted in a *New
York Times* article later that summer. This time, Newhouse
prevailed.

In November of 1934, the Guild led its first full newspaper strike in support of editorial workers at the *Newark
Ledger*. A number of employees had been fired for organizing,
so forty-five Guild reporters and editors walked out in solidarity. The Guild applied all the techniques learned during
the earlier protests: sound trucks, a competing union newspaper, banners, and marches. "I don't think there is a person in
Newark who doesn't know about this strike," wrote a reporter
covering the strike for the radical magazine *New Masses*.
"People from the curbs and from other cars which pulled up
and shouted encouragement at us."[46]

The Typographical Union, the Electrical Workers
Union, the County Cigar, Stationers, and Newspaper Dealers
Association, and other blue-collar unions shared resources
and marched alongside the Guild during the strike. The
strike only ended when a federal mediator intervened, leading the besieged owner to sell the whole enterprise to one S. I.

Newhouse. It was an anticlimactic end to the Newark strike, but the Guild had fulfilled its earliest, unstated function: to make some noise.

Over the course of 1934, Broun and his crew radically shifted the conversation among journalists, editors, and other newspaper workers. White-collar and blue-collar workers were working together.

The American Newspaper Guild joined the American Federation of Labor in 1936, cementing the relationships with blue-collar unions that Broun formed during his suburban newspaper battles. This national newspaper union joined the Communications Workers of America in 1997. Broun's local Newspaper Guild of New York evolved into the NewsGuild of New York, a local union that counts almost three thousand members and is now part of the larger Communications Workers of America union.

The first decade of the twenty-first century was not kind to unions in any profession. According to the Bureau of Labor Statistics, union membership hit a new low in 2014. Only 11 percent of American workers had union membership, compared to 20 percent of workers back in 1983. Publishing and newspapers saw major decreases as well. In 2002, 10 percent of the traditional publishing industry was represented by unions, according to the Bureau of Labor Statistics. By 2014, only 3.6 percent of all employees in this sector had union support.

Digital writing has been considered a profession for more than twenty years, but my generation of writers did not find the sense of solidarity that mobilized newspaper reporters and editors during the Great Depression until recently. Employees at Gawker Media, Salon Media, and Vice Media all organized with the Writers Guild of America, East during the course of a single year. In July 2015, staffers at the Guardian US voted to join the News Media Guild, another New York City local. By September, the digital journalists at Al Jazeera America voted to join the NewsGuild of New York, the union that evolved from Broun's Newspaper Guild of New York.

"In all, it seems like we haven't come too far since the 1930s," former Gawker editor and organizer Hamilton Nolan told me in an email, looking back at the earliest demands of the Newspaper Guild of New York. "One of the more unanimous things people here wanted to ask for is a wage scale, which we hope to get in our contract, along with a system for giving raises regularly and fairly. We are also asking for the institution of severance pay."

A year after this union victory, Hulk Hogan bankrupted Gawker founder Nick Denton with a lawsuit over a controversial post about the former wrestler's sex life. The suit got financial support from billionaire Peter Thiel, a known critic of the web network. Within days, the website Gawker had shuttered. Denton sold the rest of his blog media company to the Spanish-language TV network Univision in a $135 million fire sale. Nolan now reports for *The Splinter*, the Univision-owned website that channels the spirit of Gawker in the political scene.

Ever since the first journalists organized, unions have been blamed for destroying the publications that they protect. During one union battle of the 1930s, Newhouse raged against a group of unionized Long Island journalists: "The Newspaper Guild, in plain words, forced the patient to die by threatening the doctor with a shotgun."[47] His metaphor made for good copy, but it isn't really true.

Newhouse was never a doctor trying to save a dying patient. Like the publishers raising millions in venture capital in the aughts, Newhouse was a businessman seizing epochal opportunities. Unions unquestionably made Newhouse's life more difficult, but they never stopped him from building one of the twentieth century's greatest media empires. Above all, the journalists that Newhouse employed were not patients in need of life-saving surgery. They were workers cowed into the illusion that they were alone.

5. CORNELL WOOLRICH

Failure Is Our Business

During the 1930s, an intrepid band of authors churned out millions of words for disposable magazines printed on cheap paper. Cornell Woolrich entered the Great Depression as a promising literary star but came out on the other side of the economic disaster as a pulp fiction king, the grandfather of hardboiled noir.

While working in Los Angeles in his early twenties, Woolrich wooed Gloria Blackton, the daughter of a film mogul. Woolrich had recently won a $10,000 writing prize and wanted to be the next F. Scott Fitzgerald. They quickly eloped, swept up by the promise of his career. Those were the early days of the Great Depression, back when it seemed like it would be temporary.

According to Francis M. Nevins's biography of the pulp fiction legend, Woolrich kept a locked suitcase and a secret diary in his bedroom. Soon after they married, Gloria pried open his suitcase and found a sailor suit hidden inside. Then she read his diary, a book describing his secret life as a gay man. Many years later, her sister Marion explained in an interview: "He would don the sailor suit; get up in the night and leave her. In the dark he would put on the sailor suit and go down to the waterfront and find whatever experience he was looking for."[1]

Even after Gloria discovered the sailor suit and the diary, they didn't immediately get divorced. Instead, Woolrich sailed on a European cruise with his mother during the early 1930s. Drifting around the world, he wrote his sixth novel—a flop. He returned to the city a failure: "It was no time in which to be a writer. Magazines were expiring all over, dropping off like autumn leaves falling from trees. Who had time for books, for magazines? Who had the money to waste on fairy tales of a world that had vanished?"[2]

Separated from his wife, he lived in a lonely apartment on the Upper West Side. There, Woolrich pitched a new commercial novel to an editor he knew. It would be a love story set in Paris in 1912, a Europe that existed before World War I and the global recession. The editor promised to help sell the book and the movie rights—a life-changing deal that could perhaps salvage his career. One by one, his friends were being evicted, fired, and forced to leave the city. Woolrich went to church and begged God for help: "Dear God . . . let me have this money now, while I can still enjoy it as it should be enjoyed, to the hilt . . . Let me have it now. Now. Or not at all."[3]

In March, newly elected President Franklin Roosevelt and Congress passed the Emergency Banking Act of 1933, declaring a temporary closure of the banks in order to keep Americans from withdrawing money and ruining the economy. The audacious move actually worked. NYU Stern School of Business professor William L. Silber wrote about the Act in

2012 for the Federal Reserve Bank of New York's Economic Policy Review: "Confirmation of the turnaround in expectations came in two parts: the Dow Jones Industrial Average rose by a statistically significant 15.34 percent . . . by the end of the month, the public had returned to the banks two-thirds of the currency hoarded since the onset of the panic."[4]

Nevertheless, for three terrible days, nobody knew when the banks would open again. The poet Horace Gregory was drinking at an Upper East Side party when the president closed the banks. "Drinks were transferred from the right hand to the left, while fingers searched for change in the vest and trouser pockets," he wrote later, remembering the moment when everybody figured out they were screwed. "Everyone in New York felt as poor as everyone else,"[5] he wrote. Suddenly the party dissolved into chaos. The banks were closed and all the money was gone.

A few blocks away, Cornell Woolrich was drinking with a friend in his apartment. When news broke that the banks had shuttered, the two friends compared their savings. His friend had $16 in the bank and Woolrich had $61. Throughout the apocalyptic weekend, Woolrich kept writing the novel he thought would save his career. The experience was killing him: "The two great mutually antipathetic forces in life have never been love and death, but love and hunger. Whichever gains an ascendancy, the other suffers by it. No one cares who got the girl in the story anymore. They knew he couldn't keep her very long, nowadays."[6] When the banks reopened on Monday, Woolrich withdrew his whole savings, all $61. It only lasted him two months. His problems had only just begun.

Eventually, their separation became an outright divorce. "KISSLESS BRIDE QUITS WRITER" screamed the *New York Times* headline that nearly ruined the scrawny novelist in the spring of 1933. Below this cruel headline is the engagement picture of Gloria and Cornell Woolrich. She smiles uneasily in the photo, revealing a mouth full of perfect teeth. Woolrich looks gawky—he has outsized ears, bright red lips, a pale face, and a crooked haircut. His eyes drift off camera; he seems worn out and full of dread. *The New York Times* quotes Gloria: "My husband tricked me into marrying him . . . after I discovered this deception there was no use to carry out the sham any longer, so I left him."[7]

During this same hopeless period, his editor friend told him he couldn't sell the Paris love story that Woolrich had written. The novelist's dreams of a book and movie deal were dashed. Woolrich took the rejected manuscript to a bar and got drunk. On his way home, he buried the manuscript in a trashcan and never looked back. He wrote: "My mother is weaker than I am, God is stronger. My mother looks up to me, admires me. God certainly doesn't . . . If you see a small child fall flat and lie there on the ground bawling, and you go over there and help it back to its feet, do you detract from that child?"[8]

During the Depression, God must have seemed to take delight in pure wickedness. Woolrich was twenty-seven years old had nearly been swallowed by the abyss.

But failure is our business. More writers fail than those who "succeed," and it is how we respond to this failure that defines us in the end.

Pulp Fiction

In January 2006, I signed up to be a publishing blogger for a business-blog network. I would be one writer among a group of bloggers who were writing about topics that ranged from advertising to human resources to public relations. I decided I could handle the network's pay scale, which meant writing a 300-word post for $7.50. I had no idea what a fair price for a story might be. My magazine friends pulled down $1 a word for glossy magazines, but I had spent two years pitching stories and had only managed to land a handful of paid assignments. I wanted to be a writer so badly, but paying outlets stuck with their own staff and contract writers. There was no place to go.

I wrote my first blog post in January 2006. The blog network announced my hiring in a press release, trying to gain traction for an entire business blog network conjured out of thin air. Since 2006, the press release has been republished by hundreds of spam sites with names like "autobloginformation.com" or "onlinereadings.info" or "nextext.net" that automatically convert press releases into content.

Within days, I discovered how the economies of scale had shifted. Nobody had time or money to craft the beautiful sentences I loved so much. We would be paid the same if we spent ten minutes, an hour, or three years on a post. One year later, the company cut our pay rate in half. The blog network added "in-text" ads as well. These hyperlinks appeared automatically under valuable keywords like "write" or "blog" or "university"—dummy links that led to advertisements for other goods or services. These links effectively tricked readers into reading advertisements embedded in articles, earning angry comments from many readers.

The company, like everybody in the publishing industry, tried everything to make money on the internet: banner ads, flash ads, and roadblocks, but none if it could make enough money to keep the network afloat. Even as our pay scale declined from $7.50 per post to $4.50 per post, the blog network couldn't support itself. I watched this happen over and over at other sites and magazines: blog traffic was swelling at newspapers and websites, but nobody could produce enough ad revenue to stay afloat. At some point in 2008, the blog network stopped paying writers all together. I kept writing anyway, if only to maintain the illusion that I had a job until I found another freelance writing position.

I've never told anybody about those months that I worked for free. We all had stories we didn't share, too ashamed to admit how little we accepted for a post or a story. "Freelance content creators" could never organize because we had no idea what anybody else was making or even where they were. We worked on a virtual factory floor, but we couldn't see each other. In other words, we lived like pulp fiction writers.

In 1934, Woolrich crawled out from the wreckage of his personal and professional life, clutching his first pulp fiction story in his ragged hand. According to Nevins, the magazine *Detective Fiction Weekly* paid the writer $110 for "Death Sits in the Dentist's Chair" in May of that year. The story opens with a detective studying another patient at the dentist's office: "He was sitting there quietly, humbly, with all the terrible resignation of the very poor. He wasn't jittery and alert like I was, but just sat at the ready to take anything that came, head bowed a little as though he found life just a succession of hard knocks."[9] A few minutes later the sad man dies in the dentist's chair. The detective spends the rest of the story solving the mystery, discovering that a rival doctor poisoned the unlucky patient to ruin the career of the dentist.

The pulp fiction market imploded in the early 1930s. At the beginning of the Great Depression, there were seventy-three pulp fiction magazines, and they paid an average of two cents per word. The best writers could even make ten cents a word. By the end of the Depression, only thirty-three pulp fiction magazines survived, each paying an average of a penny a word. "There is strong competition now in the pulp market," wrote *The New York Times*, "Writers accustomed to the higher pay of the 'smooth paper' magazines have found decreasing markets for the last few years and many have entered the lower price field." Woolrich described his new lifestyle in the story "Penny-a-Worder":

> The story flowed like a torrent. The margin bell chimed almost staccato, the roller turned with almost piston-like continuity, the pages sprang up almost like blobs of batter from a pancake skillet. The beer kept rising in the glass and, contradictorily, steadily falling lower. The cigarettes gave up their ghosts, long thin gray ghosts, in good cause; the mortality rate was terrible.[10]

The pulp-fiction writers churned out word counts that seemed absurd to the next generation of writers. For many years after, the writing industry paid writers to think and craft elegant prose, buoying them with writing workshops and the expense accounts of glossy magazines. But I entered a writing market in the first decade of the twenty-first century. The market had been gutted by layoffs. We had no common pay scale, no concept of a fair workday, and no idea when we should stop writing.

Woolrich's protagonist in the short story "The Death of Me" scrawls a quick suicide note to his wife: "Sorry, old dear, too many bills." As his main character prepares to blow his brains out, Woolrich considers his protagonist's clothing: "It was one of those suits sold by the job-lot, hundreds of them all exactly alike, at seventeen or nineteen dollars a throw, and distributed around town on the backs of life's failures. It had been carrying around hundreds of dollars--in money owed. Every pocket had its bills, its reminders, its summonses."[11] The main character shoves a gun against his head, "a little above the ear." The gun jams and the narrator stumbles away to get drunk on grain alcohol.

Retail outlets were also struggling, of course. Stores tried to convince customers to spend their leftover pennies instead of hoarding them. Predatory book pricing became a weapon of major department stores during the early days of the Great Depression. In a bid to get weary consumers to start shopping again, department stores sold books at a steep discount. These loss leaders brought valuable foot traffic into the stores but threatened to cripple the publishing industry. Gutted publishers battled department stores to survive.

Publishers Weekly chronicled the ongoing price wars during these grim years. The trade publication bemoaned the "ludicrous sight" of new books selling for half the wholesale price on department store floors. "Bookstores cancelled their orders to publishers and sent their list boys to the department stores where they were able to pick up books for stock at prices considerably lower than they would have had to pay the publishers."[12]

In mid-1934, publishers and booksellers won federal protection from predatory pricing. They created a new price code, following the National Recovery Act's mandate to fight retail abuses. The booksellers were actually relieved that they didn't have to fight each other any longer: "I, for my part, however, would rather starve to death with price maintenance than be crushed to death by cut-throat competition. Price-cutting is out!" cheered one bookseller in *Publishers Weekly*. As the new year dawned in 1935, Macy's ran a massive three-column advertisement in all the New York papers, urging readers to buy books that had escaped the code: "Tomorrow over 1,200 Books Freed from Price Fixing Provisions of the Booksellers' Code . . . The self-denial their high prices have imposed on you is now in the past . . . Check this list--then hurry in to the street floor--or telephone or write or wire at once."[13]

Amazon's Price Wars

These days publishers face the same predatory pricing from the only department store left in the twenty-first century—Amazon.com. Jeff Bezos uses digital books the same way that department stores used bestselling books during the Depression. He introduced the $400 Amazon Kindle in 2007, but swiftly reduced the price to maximize the number of paying eBook customers in his audience. A version of the device can now be bought for less than $100. Analysts speculate that—at best—the company breaks even on these devices. The company makes money on eBook purchases from readers who enter the proprietary Kindle ecosystem.

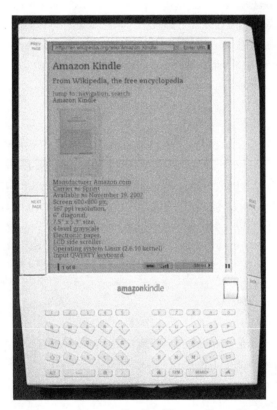

A first-generation Amazon Kindle. "Eventually, publishers will become so dependent on Amazon for distribution that they'll have to give it better terms." Photo by Jon 'ShakataGaNai' Davis, courtesy Wikimedia Commons.

At the same time, Amazon sold books for $9.99, setting an affordable but potentially disastrous precedent for publishers. A reporter at Business Insider Intelligence explained the model:

> Amazon started out by . . . losing money on e-book sales by adopting the "wholesale model": buying books from publishers at regular print wholesale prices and then selling them at a discount to set reader expectations of a lower price for e-books . . . Eventually, publishers will become so dependent on Amazon for distribution that they'll have to give it better terms.[14]

Steve Jobs softened Amazon's stranglehold on the industry in January 2010, unveiling the iPad (with a starting price of $499) and a digital bookstore that would allow publishers to control prices. For the first time, the industry started talking about fixed eBook prices instead of allowing Amazon to permanently undercut the competition with a $9.99 standard.

In February 2010, Macmillan engaged in a weeklong standoff in an attempt to force Amazon to raise their eBook prices. At the height of the conflict, Amazon yanked the "Buy Direct from Amazon" buttons off Macmillan books, cutting the publisher off completely. Macmillan CEO John Sargent took to the internet, outlining a new eBook price scale dubbed the "agency model" that priced the digital edition of first edition hardcover books between $12.99 and $14.99. Four major publishers soon followed suit. Hachette Book Group, Random House, Simon & Schuster, and HarperCollins arranged similar deals, selling digital books for the same price across all marketplaces. When the agency pricing deal took effect in 2010, Amazon responded by adding a curt "This price was set by the publisher" tag to every book priced under the new scale, sending a clear message to customers.

Amazon customers responded passionately in the Amazon forums. One customer generated 10,000 comments with a "boycott anything over $9.99" post in the forums: "It is important that Amazon and the publishers realize that they will not be selling books that are over $10. It's important that OLD and NEW Kindle folk DO NOT purchase anything over $9.99. This was one of the big selling points for me, and I will not be bait and switched." One new Kindle user complained about the quality of eBooks: "Don't expect me to pay for an e-book much over the price of the lowest priced paperback. So far what I've consistently seen of ridiculously numerous formatting errors, lack of adequate hyperlinking, and nonexistent cover art in the commercial e-books does not warrant the prices you are attempting to receive."

Amazon had the last laugh. The consumer rights firm Hagens Berman sued Apple and the five major publishers who agreed to the agency-model pricing. According to the lawsuit, the eBook pricing violated both federal and state antitrust regulations: "While free market forces would dictate that e-books would be cheaper than their hard-copy counterparts, considering lower production and distribution costs, the complaint shows that as a result of the agency model and alleged collusion, many e-books are more expensive than their hard-copy counterparts."[15] The firm speculated that damages "could total tens of millions of dollars," and a number of copycat lawsuits were filed as well by other customers.

A federal lawsuit quickly followed. In April 2012, the Department of Justice sued Apple and the five publishers that agreed on the agency model for eBook prices, arguing that "they conspired to eliminate retail price competition, resulting in consumers paying millions of dollars more for their e-books." All five of the major publishers ended up settling. These massive conglomerates cut their losses and limped out of the recession, paying millions to avoid a court battle over digital book prices. Publishers, authors, and readers debated the DOJ's strategy for months.

The DOJ Antitrust Division Chief of Staff Jamillia Ferris cheered these sinking margins in a press release regarding Macmillan's (the final publisher to strike a deal with the DOJ) settlement:

> As a result of today's settlement, Macmillan has agreed to immediately allow retailers to lower the prices consumers pay for Macmillan's e-books . . . Just as consumers are already paying lower prices for the e-book versions of many of Hachette's, HarperCollins' and Simon & Schuster's new releases and best sellers, we expect the prices of many of Macmillan's e-books will also decline.[16]

Random House and Penguin announced a merger in the fall of 2012. The new entity would be called Penguin Random House. Faced with ruthless competition from Amazon, they needed to consolidate their power to fight future battles more effectively. Apple opted to slug it out with the DOJ in court, a costly and uphill battle. In July 2013, U.S. district judge Denise Cote decided that Apple did collude with the five publishers. Apple appealed the ruling, but in the meantime, the prices of eBooks continued to sink. Three or four major corporations were fighting for razor-thin margins and the bidding rights to the next commercial blockbusters.

In May 2014, Amazon engaged in a very public conflict with the publisher Hachette. The dispute arose over confidential contract negotiations between two powerful corporations, so we will never know the exact terms of battle. When Hachette would not agree to Amazon's demands, the company began to throttle the publisher's sales through the online retailer. More than one thousand writers banded together under the name "Authors United," exposing the conflict in editorials, appearances and a letter sent to Amazon shareholders outlining the company's tactics in the battle against Hachette:

> These sanctions included refusing preorders, delaying shipping, reducing discounting, and using pop-up windows to cover authors' pages and redirect buyers to non-Hachette books . . . These sanctions have driven down Hachette authors' sales at Amazon.com by at least 50 percent and in some cases as much as 90 percent. These sales drops are occurring across the board: in hardcovers, paperbacks, and e-books. Because of Amazon's immense market share and its proprietary Kindle platform, other retailers have not made up the difference.[17]

The standoff ended in November 2014, with both companies touting that they had struck "a multi-year agreement for eBook and print sales in the US." Readers and writers will never know the exact terms or scope of the secret negotiations, but its effects will be felt for years in the publishing industry. Amazon's Kindle VP David Naggar gave a vague and cheery description of the deal: "We are pleased with this new agreement as it includes specific financial incentives for Hachette to deliver lower prices, which we believe will be a great win for readers and authors alike."[18]

At the 2014 National Book Awards, the great science fiction author Ursula Le Guin articulated her dissent against contemporary bookselling in a fiery speech. The Electronic Frontier Foundation activist Parker Higgins transcribed the speech. Le Guin blasted Amazon (one of the National Book Award sponsors) without ever saying the company's name: "We just saw a profiteer try to punish a publisher for disobedience and writers threatened by corporate fatwa, and I see a lot of us, the producers who write the books, and make the books, accepting this. Letting commodity profiteers sell us like deodorant, and tell us what to publish and what to write."

Her speech rocked the ceremony, generating headlines for the next week in the publishing world. Many applauded her candor and willingness to challenge Amazon's power, but I was haunted by a grim prophecy hidden in the speech. She warned the assembled publishers that writers will still face many challenges. She wrote: "Hard times are coming, when we'll be wanting the voices of writers who can see alternatives to how we live now, can see through our fear-stricken society and its obsessive technologies to other ways of being, and even imagine real grounds for hope."[19]

Despite the end of the Great Recession, the hard times are not over for writers. Her words reminded me why we need to read the Crisis Generation authors now, more than ever.

***

The Great Depression–era national law against predatory book pricing only lasted until May 1935 when the Supreme Court declared the "retail codes" unconstitutional. Publishers then turned to state laws, pushing for the "Feld-Crawford

Fair Trade Law," a remarkable piece of legislation that helped publishers set prices for the rest of the Great Depression.

In November 1935, Doubleday took on the founder of Macy's in the New York Supreme Court, fighting to keep the legislation alive. But Justice Frederick P. Close ruled that the Feld-Crawford Act was unconstitutional, writing: "The act attempts to give to private persons unlimited power over the property of others." The law was officially overturned in January 1936.

One year later, the publishers won an appeal and the code was reinstated. In March 1937, National Association of Book Publishers president Stanley Rinehart cheered the recently reinstated law: "The prices of the books will be established in each instance by the publishers." *The New York Times* captured the bitter dissatisfaction at the department store: "Officials of Macy's said yesterday they were availing themselves of the privileges of the Feld-Crawford law which permit the retailer having 'price fixed' merchandise on hand to offer it back to the producers."[20]

Gone with the Wind was the first book to be re-priced under the Fair Trade Law in New York. The price had dipped to 89 cents (equivalent to $14) at some stores. When publishers set the new price at $3 (equivalent to $47), Macy's promptly returned 36,000 copies of the novel to Macmillan. The publisher grudgingly accepted the bitter returns, noting "we believe . . . that, with the price of *Gone with the Wind* stabilized, its sale will go right on."[21]

They were right. The novel became one of the biggest bestsellers of the twentieth century.

The Dance

When we think of noir, we think of stylish trenchcoats, neon shadows, and gangsters, but Woolrich founded the genre of noir fiction with a story set in an empty warehouse with a busted light bulb sputtering overhead while six people danced themselves to death.

The murder mystery begins after a slew of participants in a nightmarish dance marathon end up dancing for nine days straight, each hoping to win a thousand bucks. The dance contest takes place in the middle of a New York City armory. It was a soul-crushing way to make money. Woolrich pitied the half-starved kids dancing for the contest, a century before *American Idol* and *Survivor*: "Six scarecrows, three men and three girls, clung ludicrously together in pairs in the middle of the floor. They were not dancing and they were not walking, they were tottering by now, barely moving enough to keep from standing still."[22]

During the late 1920s and early 1930s, promoters also staged grueling speaking competitions, doling out cash to the contestant who could keep talking the longest.

John Gildea, another Raven Poetry Circle member, earned a meager living at the "talk contests." Gildea made headlines for winning these public speaking marathons using poetry, reciting an endless stream of Shakespearean sonnets, his own poetry, and nonsense verse for days straight. The talk marathons took place at the 71st Regiment Armory. The massive site housed the National Guard and two other military regiments.

Milton D. Crandall promoted both dance and talk contests around the city. According to *The New York Times*, he was inspired by a legendary divorce case, a marriage that ended because the chatterbox wife talked too much.

Attendants, doctors, and dentists staffed the armory during these manic talk fests, giving audiences a peek at functional madness eighty years before reality TV. Hundreds of people would pay to watch the crazy scenes unfold, but they usually left when the marathons grew mundane and sad. The survivors ended up talking in empty rooms.

From 1933 until 1935, sickly, pallid Woolrich saw how nasty life could be: he had been outed by cruel newspaper reporters, forced to bury his failed literary novel in the trash, and forced to hide his identity as a gay man or risk more public humiliation and starvation.

His series of failures produced a bleak new kind of story.

The summer of 1935, Woolrich churned out a pulp fiction story that could only have been written during hard times: a woman calls a private detective for help but finds out he's already been laid off: "After the depresh is over everywhere else, it suddenly hits the investigation business as an afterthought. And at my age too! . . . Too old, they think! Not up-to-date enough!"[23]

The detective takes the case of the murdered socialite anyway. She has been strangled with her own dress straps at the edge of a floating dance parlor in New Jersey. She dies in the back of the pleasure boat, a shadowy corner "purposely left dark" so the dancers can make out in the darkness. "Thoughts of death must have been very far from her mind. But a noisy jazz-band can drown out the loudest scream. The tune it was pounding out was 'I'm the Boogey Man,'"[24] wrote Woolrich. Murder, love, and obsession would be forever entangled in his spooky prose.

The great crime novelist Dennis Lehane revived the lay-off noir genre in 2010 with *Moonlight Mile*. While his private detective hero still has work, he struggles as a freelance detective trying to break into the world of salaried workers.

The detective delivered a speech that seemed out of place in this tough guy genre: "I'm sucking it up, Ange, and doing jobs I don't like for a company I'm not terribly in love with so that eventually I can get hired permanent and we can get insurance and benefits and a paid vacation."[25]

Economic woes have always played a crucial role in the evolution of crime fiction. The great novelist Dashiell Hammett would help the private detective genre grow in a different way during the Great Depression: in Hammett's *The Thin Man*, a once famous detective retires, discovering boredom, alcoholism, and the deadly passions of the upper class.

While Hammett's detective leaves the working class only to find a new kind of darkness in the lives of rich New Yorkers, Lehane's hero can barely survive on the fringes of the middle class. Lehane brought the art form back to the average Joe without sacrificing the snappy dialogue or violence.

Lehane also includes all the fears and anxieties of a free-lance writer in his novel. There is a character who specializes in "black market health care": a drug dealer who helps needy people get legal drugs that they could never afford under America's system. The book also takes a parting shot at Amazon when a gangster shows off his stolen Kindle eBook readers: "I can't even give those fucking things away,"[26] he complains.

By 1936, Woolrich had a full-time career. That year he published "Death in the Air," one of his most carefully-plotted stories, setting a narrative pace that generations of new writers would aspire to match.

The story opens with the now-defunct elevated train weaving through "old mangy tenements" where Greenwich Village streets entangled with the industrial landscape of the Lower West Side. "Four out of five were tenantless, windows either boarded up or broken-glass cavities yawning at the night,"[27] he wrote.

The sleepy commute is shattered when a passenger takes a stray bullet in the face. Woolrich relishes the irony of a man killed while taking a mundane trip home, killed while hidden behind his newspaper: "Death had leaped out at him from the very print he was reading. Such-and-such, then—period! A big black one, right into the brain."[28]

My favorite sentence from "Death in the Air" could also describe Woolrich's new life: "Like a steam-roller pursuing a motorcycle; it can't keep up with it, but it can keep remorselessly after it, wear it down, slowly overtake it, and finally flatten it out."[29]

He would spend the rest of his life essentially holed up in a hotel with a typewriter, ignoring his problems. Even when he was dying in the 1950s, alone and pickled with booze, he ignored a sore festering on his foot, unable to face the wound. By the time the doctors discovered his rotting foot, they had to amputate. He died a few months after his operation.

Paperback Writers

In the middle of the Great Depression, critics told the publishing executive Edward Weeks that the publishing profession would be dead in a few years, crushed by the steamroller economics of Depression-era publishing. In response, Weeks made a number of predictions, certain that publishing could survive. "Fewer and better books,"[30] was his useful touchstone.

He was certainly not right about everything: "The sale of light fiction bound in cloth was demonstrated to be a flat failure," he wrote. He also saw "lending library tripe" as the root of publishing's problems: "the distribution of silly, warm romances—you know the titles: Hot Flesh, Bed and Bored, Two Girls In a Studio—they have definitely helped to cheapen the production of books in this country."[31]

In reality, paperbacks would change the world. Despite Weeks's predictions, the mass-market paperback would be the very solution to publishing's problems for many publishers willing to take risks.

The British publisher Allen Lane launched Penguin Books in 1935, selling penny paperback reprints. A 1937 *New York Times* profile of the paperback baron noted that when Lane first suggested the idea to a respectable publisher, "his suggestion was laughed at." Nevertheless, he managed to sell millions of his penny reprints during the economic crash, building "one of the biggest publishing enterprises in the world"[32] in the space of two years. The publisher who ignored his original pitch ended up going out of business during the same time.

World War II was actually one of the biggest forces that helped spur the growth of paperbacks in the United States. A coalition of publishers and military agencies launched the Armed Services Editions, an effort that the Antiquarian Booksellers' Association of America called "the largest book give-away enterprise in world history." Bookseller James Dourgarian wrote about the awe-inspiring publishing effort to send paperback books to our troops:

> It began in 1943 and ended in 1947. Its achievement staggers the mind. During that small time frame, more than 1,300 titles were produced. A total of nearly 123 million volumes was distributed to soldiers, all thanks to a cooperative enterprise which involved several Army and Navy agencies, the War Production Board, 70 publishing firms, and more than a dozen printing houses, composition firms, and paper suppliers.[33]

Ironically, digital books initially decimated the mass market paperback trade, gutting the format that arose in the 1930s. The digital publishing boom has inspired a seemingly limitless pool of aspiring writers. Every kind of book can now be published and circulated online; there is no way to turn back time in order to create an industry with fewer books.

However, the marketplace for digital books has hit a difficult crossroads. Mark Coker founded the digital publishing company Smashwords in 2008 during the eBook boom. While his authors experienced early success, the publisher has been warning digital book authors that the "go-go days of exponential eBook market growth" enjoyed from 2008–2012 have ended.

In a 2018 message to his customers, Coker wrote: "the supply of eBooks is growing faster than the supply of readers. Since eBooks are digital, and because virtual shelf space is unlimited at eBook retailers, it means these books never go out of print. It's great that your book will always be available, discoverable, and purchasable, but it also means that every day from this day forward you're competing against more books."[34]

I would never discourage aspiring self-published writers who dream of following John Locke or Amanda Hocking. But they need to realize that the market will forever be saturated, for better or for worse, as long as the internet still works.

The future belongs to a scattered constellation of small publishers operating on shoestring budgets while major publishers focus on major writers, sure bets, and celebrity memoirs. This leaves the vast majority of authors competing for diminishing resources. The penny-a-worder days that Woolrich endured have returned. And according to experts like Coker, they might be here to stay.

INTERLUDE
"Pushing the Right Button"

The Depression-era self-help author Napoleon Hill despised public education, citing Thomas Edison and Henry Ford as titans of industry who never graduated from traditional schools. "Today a minimum standard of formal education is necessary to get a good start in the world of business," he wrote, recalling a fiery speech Ford once delivered to critics drawing attention to his ignorance. According to the self-help guru, Henry Ford saw education as unnecessary in our technological age:

> I have a row of electric push-buttons on my desk, and by pushing the right button, I can summon to my aid men who can answer ANY question I desire to ask concerning the business to which I am devoting most of my efforts. Now, will you kindly tell me, WHY I should clutter up my mind with general knowledge, for the purpose of being able to answer questions, when I have men around me who can supply any knowledge I require?[35]

Why should brilliant businessmen bother with public education when they can make enough money to pay somebody else to be smart? Hill's twisted logic seems even more frightening in the twenty-first century, as some of our country's most powerful companies are finding ways to automate and replace human intelligence altogether.

In 2009, Northwestern School of Journalism students teamed up with the computer science department to build a narrative algorithm capable of replacing a writer. According to *The New York Times*, twenty companies used the service in 2011, but only two were identified by name— the trade publisher Hanley Wood and the sports journalism site *The Big Ten Network*. Hanley Wood digital media and market intelligence unit president Andrew Reid told *The New York Times*: "The company had long collected the data, but hiring people to write trend articles would have been too costly."[36]

This tool can computerize a breathtaking range of writing: sports stories, financial reports, real estate analyses, local community content, polling and elections, advertising campaign summaries sales, operations reports, and market research. Here's an excerpt from an actual *Big Ten News* article generated by the program: "Wisconsin jumped out to an early lead and never looked back in a 51-17 win over UNLV on Thursday at Camp Randall Stadium. The Badgers scored 20 points in the first quarter on a Russell Wilson touchdown pass, a Montee Ball touchdown run and a James White touchdown run. Wisconsin's offense dominated the Rebels' defense."[37]

By 2014, a computer algorithm at the *Los Angeles Times* could churn out a story about an overnight earthquake— beating human journalists with the scoop about the early morning tremor. Perhaps someday robots will cover stock market crashes, natural disasters, and all other human catastrophes with the same efficiency.

In February 2019, Open AI unveiled GPT2, an artificial intelligence model that can write infinite fictional and news stories based on the logic of a few sentences from a news story or short story. The monster artificial intelligence absorbed 40 gigabytes of text—roughly the storage space of 22,000 digital books—training itself on a corpus of articles and links that received three or more "karma" votes from human beings. The data scientists called this vote tally "a heuristic indicator for whether other users found the link interesting, educational, or just funny."

Piggybacking on the labors of human readers, the company shaped an artificial intelligence model that could create imitations of human writing. Then, in a bit of PR theatrics, the company decided not to turn the model public because it could theoretically be used to write millions of reviews for a product, outing fill comments sections with nearly intelligible text. There were many other ways it could be abused. "There are many more people than us who are better at thinking what it can do maliciously,"[38] wrote Jack Clark, head of policy at Open AI.

We began the AI revolution worrying about how it could take writers' jobs, but this poses an even darker scenario. One day, AI could overrun our digital communications, flooding our libraries, e-commerce sites, and social media sites with cleverly faked writing. GPT2 produced writing compelling enough to beat spam filters and dupe millions of readers. Once that kind of literary weapon is loosed on the world, nothing digital will be untouched.

The creators shared examples of the AI's elegant nonsense. They would feed the AI a few lines of text and let the

AI sort out the appropriate tone and content for a response with help from algorithms precisely calibrated to track the rhythms of human interaction. The AI was able to learn the shape, if not the sense, of real writing.

One prompt in particular made me more fearful than the others. It began with a prompt that any Internet troll could have typed in any random comment section online: "Recycling is good for the world. NO! YOU COULD NOT BE MORE WRONG!!"[39] This was a casual, pretty much completely agreed-upon shared belief among most readers. The giant capital letters are the emotional shorthand of troll discourse online. The shrill tone touches something deep in our monkey brain. It is a shot-of-adrenaline line that incites the reader to possibly respond with the same all-caps urgency.

In other words, OpenAI fed the artificial intelligence a mundane replica of one of the many stupid and dangerous arguments going on at any given moment in millions of online discussions around the world. They could have just as easily written a prompt like "VACCINATIONS ARE EVIL" or "JEWS CONTROL GLOBAL FINANCE" to test the AI's capabilities.

The neural model returned one of the most frightening responses I've ever read, a mini-manifesto of complete falsehood which has the casual ring of a human being talking reasonably about a favorite food or football team. The model internalized the dissent—the all-caps insanity—and spat out a reasonable sounding response. The machine replied:

> Recycling is NOT good for the world. It is bad for the environment, it is bad for our health, and it is bad for our economy. I'm not kidding. Recycling is not good for the

environment. It is destructive to the earth and it is a major contributor to global warming.[40]

Anti-vaccination activists could spam every single Facebook user with a similar anti-vaccination argument customized to include social media details from that particular user. Anti-Semites could send personalized emails to every person on earth, with the AI seamlessly combining personal beliefs with reasonable-sounding calls for genocide.

These questions go far beyond just the fortunes of writers. In 2012, Amazon bought Kiva Systems, a robot maker that designs tools for handling goods inside vast Amazon warehouses. Amazon paid $775 million to acquire the company. Amazon has been investing in a future where they no longer need so many pesky humans, hoping to lead an economic revolution that all competitors must follow.

In an essay called "Robots in 2015," Marshall Brain predicts that such robots will cause unemployment rates of unprecedented proportions:

> Any company that does not automate will be at such a pricing disadvantage that it will go out of business. Ten million unemployed workers dumped onto the job market over the course of five years will have a profound effect on the unemployment statistics in the United States. The problem is that this same sort of thing will be happening in every sector of the economy at a very rapid pace, dumping millions more unemployed workers onto the job market at the same time.[41]

Before all of these headlines broke, we were already used to a workplace reduced by automation: hundreds of thousands of jobs, from travel agents to assembly line workers to secretaries to mail delivery, were all being sucked into the nebulous land of technological obsolescence.

Some look forward to a life of shared leisure in our automated future, but Henry Ford's example demonstrates the way that already-powerful moguls will always monopolize intelligence. In the twenty-first century, we have absorbed these momentous technological shifts without ever finding a balance for workers.

When the Crisis Generation faced that same struggle, they fought back with strikes. A *New Masses* essay from 1934 called out factories for exploiting workers, even though productivity had multiplied as a result of technology:

> If a single worker can now produce 30 times as much as a worker used to produce in the nineteenth century, that means the economic and social importance of that worker has increased approximately 30 times . . . the rising productivity of the worker is an index of his increased exploitation. It is also a measure of the effectiveness with which the workers can strike back at the capitalists. All the strikes of the past two years bear out this important point.[42]

Our twenty-first-century push-button machines will only make their rich creators richer. These machines will do our jobs, but the Henry Fords of the world will never worry about finding new work for the replaced humans.

6. KENNETH FEARING

"And Wow He Died As Wow He Lived"

During the decadent final years of the Roaring Twenties, Kenneth Fearing burst onto the literary scene with his reckless and stylized first book, *Angel Arms*. The strongest pieces were free-form riffs on hard-boiled fiction themes: "dangerous, handsome, cross-eye'd Louie the rat / Spoke with his gat, Rat-a-tat-tat—"

But a majestic and revolutionary spirit was balanced against these staccato pieces, like this stanza from "Ballad of the Salvation Army":

> On Fourteenth Street the bugles blow,
> Bugles blow, bugles blow,
> The torpid stones and pavements wake,
> A million men and streetcars quake
> In time with angel breasts that shake,
> Blow, bugles, blow.

Fearing's apocalyptic imagery proved timely. Within months of the publication of *Angel Arms,* the stock market crashed, taking the fortunes of the literary world with it. Fearing submerged himself in alcohol. The journalist Joseph Mitchell

"Ghost out of ghost out of ghost." A few unemployed workers set up a ragged Christmas tree outside a Twelfth Avenue shack during the Great Depression. Photograph by Russell Lee, courtesy the Library of Congress.

profiled the poet during these boozy days: "he sought for and always found the bottoms of countless bottles of empathetic Prohibition gin . . . He became a sort of symbol. He was 'the drunken poet.' He was 'a crazy guy.'"

Fearing wrote pulp fiction, porn, and poems for a few years, scraping together a living for his family. *Angel Arms* barely registered in the critical press. According to his first wife, Rachel Meltzer, "his shirts . . . were green with grime, his teeth covered with tartar." Rachel brought in the household's only steady paycheck, working while her husband wrote. The scholar Robert M. Ryley noted that Fearing's wife "would get so tired that, much to Fearing's annoyance, she would fall asleep at parties." Fearing is parodied in Albert Halper's 1933 novel *Union Square*: "'Blow, bugles, blow,' he mumbled sloppily, 'and answer, hot dogs, answer, wharking, jarking, karking. On Fourteenth Street the mustard's green, in Union Square the mob is queen. Blow, bugles, blow, set the wild echoes barking. And answer, comrades, answer, harking, larking, farking.'"

The same year, Fearing published the poem "1933" in the *New Masses*. In his poem, stolen stocks and bonds are rescued and criminals are fruitlessly captured and released: "ghost out of ghost out of ghost . . . saw ten million dead returned to life, shot down again, again restored . . . Inexorably, the thief was pursued. Captured inexorably. Tried. Inexorably acquitted."

The poem mocked popular culture's cycle of distress and redemption. Over and over again, pulp fiction, radio dramas, and newsreels manufactured easy answers to daunting problems. In the post-apocalyptic New York City of 1933, popular culture struggled to stimulate a revival of the fortunes of the twenties through sheer optimism. This naive impulse only made things worse for those sensitive to reality.

Kenneth Fearing sobered up in 1934 and set about writing his masterpiece, a skinny collection called simply *Poems*. In an interview with Joseph Mitchell, he talked about his new work: "The thing about these poems is that they express my indignation over such things as that jungle of squatters over on Abingdon Square and people I see at night going around the streets at night like prehistoric animals, digging into garbage pails, a sight which epitomizes our so-called civilization."

Alice Neel painted a surrealistic portrait of Fearing. In the painting, the thirty-three-year-old stares at us through owl-rimmed glasses. His eye sockets are hollow from exhaustion and hunger. There is a gaping hole in Fearing's chest: a grinning skeleton is perched inside, spilling a bucket of blood.

During 1933, the *New Masses* published six of Fearing's poems, even though the magazine ran less than one poem a week. He would ultimately publish more than thirty pieces in the magazine, finding a new audience as the Depression dragged onward. Unlike many other poets, Fearing's wild experiments had a target. His poetry went straight after Wall Street. He made collages that strung together snatches of protest signs, Wall Street tickers, sad Depression stories, and newspaper slogans—the stories of the 99 percent living in the 1930s.

Kenneth Fearing couldn't find a publisher for *Poems*. The Depression had wiped out any resources at publishers for mid-list or radical writers at the fringe of the industry. Instead, Fearing decided on the unusual strategy of raising money through subscriptions to publish his book.

In April 2009, in the deep dark middle of our own crash, a company called Kickstarter opened for business online. The model was simple: writers, journalists, artists, and filmmakers could pitch a project to potential fans, estimating how much money they would need to complete the project. If they could raise enough pledges, they would receive money from these backers.

By the summer of 2011, Kickstarter counted 26,620 attempted projects. Only 10,388 of those projects actually met their funding goal, but the service provided a brand new financing outlet for creative people. In a time when grants, government art funding, and patronage shrank to disastrous levels, this new tool seemed to be helping writers survive.

But the company is not entirely free of corporate influence. Kickstarter got started by using Amazon to handle credit card payments in the United States, giving them a cut of every successfully funded project. Kickstarter has also received investment from prominent Silicon Valley venture capitalists, including the co-founders of influential companies like Twitter, Vimeo, and Flickr.

Fearing printed one thousand copies of *Poems* and created an accidental poetry bestseller. His new work blasted the bankers, fat cats, and politicians who plunged the country into an economic dark age. The bombastic "Dirge" dishes out comic-book style retribution: "Wham, Mr. Roosevelt; pow, Sears Roebuck; awk, big / dipper; bop, summer rain; / Bong, Mr., bong, Mr., bong, Mr., bong."

The pop hymn mocks and mourns the domesticity of J. Alfred Prufrock in Fearing's most famous stanza:

And wow he died as wow he lived,

Going whop to the office and blooie home to sleep

And biff got married and bam had children and

Oof got fired

Zowie did he live and zowie did he die

During this same period, Orrick Johns hired Fearing to work on the Federal Writers Project.

Fearing thrived as an FWP staffer, uniting the fractious collection of authors and radicals. According to his former supervisor Jerre Mangione, Fearing "was one of the project's most popular staff members and had friends in all camps."

Early in his career, Fearing was pigeonholed as a "proletarian poet," but he avoided taking sides in political debates (something that probably helped him at the FWP). When FBI agents asked if he was a Communist, the poet replied: "Not yet." For years, scholars have debated his true ideological stance during these difficult days. Maybe he didn't have one at all.

Here, Fearing reached the pinnacle of his poetic career: praised as an exemplary FWP member, he earned a Guggenheim Fellowship and landed a contract with Random House. Sadly, his good luck wouldn't last.

Poets of the Great Recession

During our own economic collapse, the poet Eileen R. Tabios founded a site called "Poets Reflect on the Great Recession." The Filipino-American poet, author, and publisher curated this work with a simple mission: "this blog will feature poets presenting the ways they have been affected by the Great Recession, and how such has affected (or not) their poetry."

Unlike many poets, Tabios graduated with an MBA in economics and international business from New York University. She was a banker. Her specialty was analyzing the "financial viability" of various projects, including "energy, mining, transportation, or waste disposal infrastructure." In a description of her work, she explains:

> My analysis was not solely financial or economic; I also evaluated such factors as political stability, oceanic weather, and currency risks. I even had to evaluate Force Majeure—"Acts of God"—and determine how to protect projects against such elements as hurricanes, typhoons, and other metaphorical acts of an enraged god.

In 2001, the banker turned into a publisher. She founded Meritage Press that year, and began to release between one and four books of poetry yearly. As the recession wore on, however, she was forced to reduce her publishing output. Undaunted, she refused to stop publishing and promoting poetry:

> For (too) many artists, economic pressures can dampen the ability to continue making art. I don't wish to have the recession affect my commitment to writing/making poems. Poetry and art, unlike how many people—and unfortunately that includes (would-be) educators or those setting education policy—believe and enact, is not a luxury. For me to sacrifice poetry to economic pressures would be among the greatest blows that could be inflicted by the Great Recession—and I will battle against it.

On her site, the publisher explained how she began selling her jewelry to finance new books. She was pawning her belongings for art. The website includes photographs of the jewelry she traded for her books, such as a necklace hung with miniature charms: a butterfly, a fish, initials and a broken heart, all of it stamped in gold: "I'd been planning on keeping that necklace which, while I hadn't worn such in two decades, once meant a lot to me during my high school days. But, nowadays, sentiment can be a luxury. And I am lucky: I am not, after all, selling gold for food. Gold for Poetry. Ultimately, I don't mind: I consider Poetry to be priceless."

One of the poets that contributed to the site, Mary Krane Derr, admitted that she had spent her whole life in "low-income" situations, so the recession seemed like a relatively normal lifestyle. She confessed to planning how to save her writing materials if her family ended up evicted: "I morbidly wonder how I will lug around my laptop and journals and protect them from the snow and rain if I ever become homeless."

Her poem, "THE NIGHT BEFORE CHRISTMAS, SINGLE MOM EDITION," tackled the problem of Santa Claus:

> last thing I want
> my son to believe
> is that gifts all get here
> from some old white dude
> in a loud red suit who breaks and enters,
> breaks and enters
> all the damned night long,
> that's a Class 3 Felony,
> multiple counts.

Ed Go's poem "american" focused on the way immigrant families save food:

> (my father being from some "3rd world" we never
> threw away after a meal
> [i learned that in the lunch room])

These poets identified with the working class and were a different kind of writer from those who usually get noticed. Tabios left the site submissions open to any poet who would answer three simple questions: What is your Great Recession experience? How has the Great Recession affected your poetry? Share a poem addressing your Great Recession experience.

The final poet added to the site was Mike Berger, who wrote that he "dipped heavily into my savings to keep my kids from starving" during the Great Recession. He posted a narrative poem "Charade," the story of a blue-collar worker scarred by the economic downturn, a character that could have escaped from a Kenneth Fearing poem. Berger wrote:

> Emasculating; Bob's self-worth went
> south with the failing economy. He lost
> the spark in his eyes. He hid behind a
> pasted on smile.

***

Kenneth Fearing never quite recovered from the Great Depression. In 1938 he published the poetry collection *Dead Reckoning*, but it didn't get the same reception as his previous work. "[He] was content to repeat the earlier successes of his writing with slight variations on a central theme," wrote the poet Horace Gregory in a review.

Fearing found more fame as a novelist in the 1940s, writing a string of novels that climaxed in *The Big Clock* in 1946. Ray Milland starred in the classic film noir adaptation of the book, which eclipsed the fame that Fearing's poetry once enjoyed.

Dead Reckoning included the poem "Literary," a sarcastic advertisement from an imaginary writing school brochure.

Fearing rails against "The Literary System" that provides:

[a] thousand noble answers to a thousand empty

questions, by a patriot who needs the dough.
And so it goes.
Books are the key to magic portals. Knowledge is

power. Give the people light.
Writing must be such a nice profession.
Fill in the coupon. How do you know? Maybe you

can be a writer, too.

Fearing's poem skewered one of the most misguided myths about writers: that writers are trying to write the next great American novel or next smash-hit movie script in order to get rich. Writers know better than anyone that they haven't chosen the most lucrative profession. That doesn't mean they still don't want a fair wage and maybe some affordable health insurance.

After his second marriage dissolved in 1952, Fearing spent the last years of his life in his bachelor apartment. He drank pints of whisky every day, cobbling together a living as a publicist, book reviewer, and, once again, as a pulp writer. Without the solidarity of the *New Masses*, without the care of Johns, and without the particular battles of the Depression, he lost the fight against the bloody skeleton inside. He died in 1961.

INTERLUDE
"To Save the Little Poets from the Gutter"

Even though many writers' reputations never survived the undertow of the Great Depression, the Federal Writers Project did manage to rescue a few of our greatest writers during this difficult time. Historian David A. Taylor wrote about the period in *Soul of a People: The WPA Writers' Project Uncovers Depression America*. In an interview, he summed up the project's tangible legacy: "It provided an unexpected incubator for talent that was otherwise idled by the Depression. The project gave some of the best writers of the twentieth century their first jobs as writers at a crucial time."

The folklore unit where May Swenson and Anca Vrbovska worked included a young writer named Ralph Ellison. The aspiring author used the folklore project as a way to capture and master the language around him on the streets of Harlem. For one project, Ellison found an elderly black man on a park bench and recorded the old man's speech, word for word:

> Today you hear all these folks got millions of dollars talking bout God. They aint fooling nobody, though. They even got "IN GOD WE TRUST" on all the silver money. But it dont mean nothing. This sun and air is God's. It dont

belong to nobody and caint no few get it all to theyself. People around this park can have all they want. But you wait. God's gonna straighten it all out. Look at the dust blowing in that wind. Thats the way all the money they got gonna be. You see things, folks, they call white, but man aint got no idea of how white God gon make things. Money wont be worth no moren that dust blowing on the ground. Wont be no men down to Washington making fifty-thousand dollars a week and folks caint hardly make eighteen dollars a month. Evervbodyll be equal, in God's time. Wont be no old man Rockerfeller, no suh! Today you caint even buy a job if you had the money to do it with.

The magnificent monologue careened from alternative history to biblical fables to newspaper stories in great huffy breaths, all delivered with the wit and poise of a Southern preacher. Ellison would channel these experiences into *The Invisible Man*. His hero would explore Harlem, encountering all of the poverty, anger, and politics that Ellison saw while working for the folklore project.

The project also sustained Claude McKay, a great poet and scholar who nearly self-destructed during the Great Depression. The Jamaican immigrant thrived in the 1920s as a globetrotting intellectual, lecturing in Paris, Berlin, Morocco, and Moscow. The year the stock market crashed, he won a William A. Harmon Foundation Gold Medal for "voic[ing] in tragic force many of the deeper feelings of the modern Negro." But as the Depression deepened, he found himself begging his friends for money. His anger surfaces in a 1934 poem called "New York:"

The city's monster advertising cries
It's manufactures spreading piling high,
Weaving Manhattan's glorious fantasies.

The radios spit. The air is charged with selling,
Even the empty puny words we utter:
Who'll take a song, our hoisted signs are yelling,
To save the little poets from the gutter?
Oh we who have sometimes felt as free as air—
Mad poets drunk with sounds of drums and flutes,
Fooling ourselves that words were precious, rare—
Our thoughts, our dreams are little prostitutes.

The FWP hired McKay a year later, rescuing him from the brink of destitution. Scholar Wayne F. Cooper explained the parameters of McKay's new job in his biography: "[H]is workday often consisted of briefly discussing his assignments with his administrative superiors and then returning home to work on his book." McKay stayed with the project for three years, savoring the free time to work on his memoir, "A Long Way from Home." His WPA efforts produced an archive of research about African American communities, including "dozens of biographical sketches on notable Harlemites."

McKay's short poem "Lenox Avenue" can be found in the FWP's *New York Almanac*. McKay reveals how his FWP work changed him, inverting his oppressive vision of Manhattan. McKay would later revise the poem, but the 1937 draft paints an inspiring picture of a bustling street corner in Harlem:

And all my senses seize the luring crowd,
Intoxicated with the common street,
The rare vernacular, laughter ringing loud,
The rhythmic movement of my people's feet.

Lost manuscripts haunted everyone in the Crisis Generation. The Raven poet Vincent Beltrone claimed he lost years' worth of poetry in a loft fire. His name only survives in *The*

Raven Poetry Anthology and the newspaper clippings where he explained how he defended the honor of a teenaged poet abducted by a con man.

Many of the Ravens share similar stories of doomed manuscripts: Gildea's crazed poetry readings, d'Harcourt's unpublished science fiction novel, Bodenheim's lost movie scripts, Egris's ghost poems, and Joe Gould's mythical "oral history," which was supposedly hidden in different corners of the city.

During their highly publicized love affair, the Prince D'Harcourt wrote a poem for Krist—a melancholy meditation on love and a weak charm against looming obscurity:

Someday in the distant future

when you look back upon a sea of vanished time

And the unseen pedals of a rose that never bloomed

Fall slowly in the dark like saddest tears,

the stillness of the abyss of love that was denied

Will be your rosary, my adorable Madonna.

We are the readers he dreamed of, rediscovering his words "upon a sea of vanished time." These writers weren't trying to make a living with poetry. But they were desperately seeking readers. They were desperately seeking a way to live forever in history; to cross the abyss. To say something that mattered to someone who cared.

7. MURIEL RUKEYSER

A Poet Takes Flight

Muriel Rukeyser's father made his fortune selling cement. He was a major developer in New York City during the booming 1920s. Her family enjoyed a country club membership, a Long Island beach house, and a chauffeur. Then, in 1932, her family went bankrupt as the housing market evaporated. Her father pulled his daughter out of Vassar two years early, and the nineteen-year-old girl decided to become a poet. Rukeyser moved home with her parents. While writing her first poems, she started hanging around with the Communist-affiliated National Students League and working odd jobs.

One year later, Rukeyser joined a carload of students headed south to cover a controversial trial, the infamous Scottsboro case in Alabama. The case had captivated the press for years. Nine African American boys were accused of gang-raping two white girls on a train. Now, these nine children were awaiting execution on death row. The National Guard had to stand guard outside the courtroom to prevent a lynching.

Once the boys were convicted of the crime, a coalition of radicals and intellectuals mounted a passionate defense.

The appeal went all the way to the Supreme Court and the boys spent many years in prison and courtrooms while fighting to clear their names. Rukeyser and her friends sat in the courtroom, parading with other activists and interviewing anybody she could about the case. Her crew made *New York Times* headlines as the situation devolved in Alabama: at the height of the trial, a Decatur policeman arrested them at midnight for the crime of hanging out with black people. A patrolman spotted these young writers interviewing African Americans in a segregated corner of Decatur and rounded them all up "for investigation." The police confiscated Rukeyser's pamphlets.

The entire crew was arraigned, and the judge sent them home without more jail time. However, Rukeyser contracted typhoid fever in the overcrowded jail. "We did not go to Decatur to agitate, but to report," she wrote in a letter defending their actions to the *New York Times*. The radicals ran out of money as they headed north. Flat broke and sick, she called her parents to beg for enough money to make it home. As soon as she was back home, she attempted to weave her interviews, impressions, and newspaper articles into lyric poetry:

Nine dark boys spread their breasts in Alabama
Schooled in the cells, fathered by want.
Mother : one writes : they treat us bad. If they send us
Back to Kirby jail, I think I shall kill myself.
I think I must hang myself by my overalls.[1]

For the next few years, the poet lived with her parents. Rukeyser's parents had nicknamed her "little elephant," mocking the young writer for her weight, favoring her baby sister who lived a more traditional life. She said that her father held the incident against her for the rest of his life. In 1935, Rukeyser cobbled together enough money for flight school. She never managed to finish the course. She was always running out of money before she could log enough hours. Nevertheless, flying became a vital metaphor for her career. She named her first book *Theory of Flight*.

During the 1930s, she felt pressure from society to abandon writing and get a real job. In an interview with the historian Monty Noam Penkower, she described how writers were viewed during the Great Depression: "the public saw them as trash ... Living meant going to the office. That meant acceptance, money and the proper capitalist virtues." Her book feels contemporary, and her words are still potent nearly a hundred years later. In "Theory of Flight," imagery unfolds like a dream sequence from an Alfred Hitchcock movie.

> We were a generation of grim children
> leaning over bedroom sills, watching
> the music and the shoulders and how the war was over,
> Laughing until the blow on the mouth broke night
> wide out from its cover.[2]

In 1935, Rukeyser joined the Writers Union, signing a petition to Franklin Roosevelt about the state of American writers. The letter begged the president to make sure that WPA funds that were putting three million other Americans back to work also went to writers:

> The mechanic walks the streets no longer. He again hears the hum of machinery. The carpenter uses his hammer and saw. The clerk, the accountant, the truckman, the ditch-digger, the road-builder and the mason—all these have work. But 800 writers have no work. One of them, in despair, has already committed suicide. We know you

do not intend, Mr. President, that a man is condemned
merely because he does not work with his hands.[3]

When the Federal Writers Project was first authorized, the
Writers Union marched alongside hundreds of now forgot-
ten radicals: the League of American Writers, the Authors
League, the Newspaper Guild, and the Yiddish Writers
Union.

They were joined by the League for the Unemployed
Physically Handicapped. All of these groups occasionally
tussled with the cops outside the WPA building. They told
reporters that they faced police brutality on the picket lines,
shouting "We want jobs!" as they circled the block.

Documentary Poetry

In 1936, the political activity swirling around the country inspired a vivid kind of experimental poetry. Rukeyser
exchanged her lyrical exploration for electrified documentary
poetry—inventing an entire genre in her early twenties.

During the 1930s, hundreds of African American
migrant workers died in Gauley, a West Virginia mining
town. They had been drilling a tunnel for two years, cutting a three-mile-long swath of ground to channel water to
a hydroelectric plant. Many had been buried anonymously
after dying of various lung ailments, and the Union Carbide
Company worked hard to keep their deaths secret. After too
many lives were lost, the cover-up collapsed: a Congressional
inquiry revealed that the workers had drilled through poisonous silica deposits and that many of them had been working
with little or no face-mask protection. The dust corroded their
lungs, killing these young miners at an incredible rate.

Rukeyser and a friend drove to Gauley in March of 1936. The duo planned on shooting a documentary about this disastrous mining operation. The film fizzled, but Rukeyser, like a Depression-era Erin Brockovich, brought back reams of interviews and notes. The epic trip laid the foundation for Rukeyser's masterpiece, *U.S. 1* (1938). The book opens with an epic documentary poem about the mining disaster—fusing television-news-camera perspective, congressional testimony, stock news, doctor reports, and oral history into a nonfiction collage. This poem became one of the most controversial and generation-defining poems of the era.

Her poem captured the voices of miners like Mearl Blankenship, a dying man who woke up gagging on his corroded lungs every night: "in the dream I always see: the tunnel choked the dark wall coughing dust."[4] Rukeyser interviewed a mother who lost her three young sons to silica poisoning. Her husband and children would bathe after work, leaving the tub coated in silica dust. Her sons died. Over and over, Rukeyser reminded the reader of the grinding poverty in these migrant communities, hammering home the impact of the economic problems that forced an entire generation of African American men to march into these death tunnels.

Rukeyser framed the whole poem like the journey of Orpheus: "He shall not be diminished, never; / I shall give mouth to my son,"[5] says the mother who lost her family in the mines, promising to tell his story. In the poem, she copied a newspaper Wall Street ticker, recording the stock value of Union Carbide inside the poem—indicting the mining company for placing shareholders' investment above the lives of its workers.

In the twenty-first century, poet Susan Briante used this Depression-era literary device to build a new kind of collage. She told me that she "fell in love" with Rukeyser when she read this section, recognizing the powerful tool inside this early documentary poem:

> These numbers, a series of high/low and opening/closing stock prices for Union Carbide, the company whose exploitative mining practices in Gauley Bridge, West Virginia, resulted in the death of an estimated 475 to 2,000 miners, provide a key to Rukeyser's whole poem. Those numbers were more important than workers' lives. The drive for profit caused the tragedy that Rukeyser so eloquently investigates in the poem. Those numbers haunted me.

In the spring of 2009, Briante began to conjure the spiritual shape of the stock market. She typed the abstract number into digital libraries, quotation collections, and algorithmic search engines. These searches uncovered quotes from classic literature seemingly encoded by the mysterious Dow.

> I allow those texts to exert their influence over a series of poems, much in the way the closing number of the Dow exerts an influence over our lives," she summarized. "I wanted to show how that same drive for Wall Street profits—those numbers--caused the economic disaster and dictated the terms of our recovery. That's how I came up with the idea of letting the daily closing number of the Dow have an impact on a poem that was written for each day.

During the 2008 crash, we all performed similar rituals, frantically checking the stock market reports as if these esoteric figures—controlled by computer-driven deals too complex for the human mind to follow—could tell us something about our lives.

The year 1936 was an important one for the documentary genre. The director Pare Lorentz was assigned to document the causes of the Dust Bowl storms that destroyed miles of farmland in the Great Plains. The film had been commissioned by the Resettlement Administration. Eventually, *The Plow That Broke the Plains* hit theaters around the country.

As with the ambitions of the FWP Guidebook series, the government hoped to showcase New Deal achievements while simultaneously funding a great filmmaker. According to the *Encyclopedia of the Great Plains*, Lorentz's film was shown in independent theaters, school auditoriums, and other public meeting places throughout the country. It was seen by 10 million people in 1937 alone and the encyclopedia dubbed the radical documentary "one of the most widely viewed films in American history."[6]

The documentary begins with a theatrical narrator reading his lines with the force of an Old Testament prophet: "High winds and sun. High winds and sun. A country without rivers and with little rain." The narrator repeats that phrase like a biblical incantation throughout the documentary. Cattle march across a massive plain like ants. In one shot, the camera tilts to take in massive cloud castles looming over a sliver of grasslands below.

Through a mixture of documentary footage and reenactments, the film shows a sharecropper family being evicted, fleeing dust storms in a battered truck: "Blown out. Baked out and broke. Nothing to stay for and nothing to hope for. Homeless. Penniless and bewildered, they joined the great army of the highway."

The movie maps the transition from hand tools to farm machines, a mighty montage moving from one-horse plows to wood threshers: "The next generation of wheat will win the war!" cheers the narrator, screaming at the top of his lungs as a brigade of tractors streams across fields, dust growing thicker and thicker while machine guns clatter in the background. In the climactic montage, the director intercuts tank footage from Europe with industrial farming footage from America. "Wheat will win the war," yells the narrator, tilting out of control as veterans return triumphantly from the war and tractors with giant combustion engines steer along the fields.

Rukeyser's poem "The Book of the Dead" opens with the same epic sweep as *The Plow That Broke the Plain*. The poem is narrated with the same camera-lens precision, including pans, montages, and dissolves. The poet even reflects the camera lens back at the reader:

> Camera at the crossing, sees the city
> A street of wooden walls and empty windows,
> The doors shut handless in the empty street,
> And the deserted Negro standing on the corner[7]

Over the forty lines of the opening stanza, the word "glass" repeats: "camera-glass," "panes of glass," "public glass," "April-glass-tinted," "plate glass window," and "beer glass," all reminding us of the young poet's camera-like eye tracking the bombed out landscape.

It's hard to imagine a documentary like *The Plow That Broke the Plains* these days—it is even harder to imagine a poet taking up the call of documentary poetry.

"The Poem Is the Fact"

Months after her trip to West Virginia, Rukeyser sailed to Spain to cover the People's Olympiad, a symbolic anti-fascist protest against the real Olympics being held in Nazi Germany. On the trip, she fell in love with a German athlete named Otto Boch. General Franco's bloody civil war began that same year, turning the Spanish countryside into a major battle zone. After witnessing skirmishes, snipers, and sacked churches, the poet was forced to evacuate without her lover. He would die in the war, haunting her poetry for the next fifty years.

She left Spain with a boatload of journalists and embassy workers just as Europe's bloody struggle with fascism began. She waved goodbye to her lover as the boat left the dock on the eve of the Spanish Civil War. She floated away on a cruise ship intended for two hundred passengers; it sank low in the water, loaded with five hundred evacuees. They floated without lights through the Mediterranean while machine guns, bombs, and surveillance planes thundered along the shoreline.

Rukeyser immortalized the experience in "Mediterranean," an elegy for her lover and for the Spanish revolutionaries. She saw herself as an emotional camera, her imagery keeping her steady in contrast to her fragile human thoughts. "the poem is the fact, memory fails / under and seething lifts and will not pass."[8]

In November, Muriel Rukeyser returned to New York City, bearing witness to the violence that she saw in Spain, the blasted churches and the snipers mowing people down who were walking the streets. She addressed a conference of two hundred women raising funds for the embattled Spanish loyalists fighting Franco's violent rebellion in Spain: "the war there now is one of humans against guns...if the women of Spain can still face the great odds against them, then we must help them in their fight for democracy."[9]

Muriel Rukeyser earned a three-page *New Masses* feature in 1937 that printed her whole epic poem. The work was illustrated by haunting art from some of the magazine's greatest artists. Social realist artist Sylvia Wald created a charcoal sketch that traced the outlines of the refugee women escaping the civil war with their belongings stuffed into boxes. The soft shape of one woman's pregnant belly drove the image. The women are brave and powerful as they head into an uncertain future. Chicago artist Henry Simon contributed a lithograph of mourning peasants standing like statues in the outskirts of a bombed out village. Beside the art, one Spanish refugee meets the poet on the street, begging her to carry these stories back to the United States. "your job is: go tell your countries what you saw in Spain."[10]

Adrienne Rich wrote a long tribute to Rukeyser called "Beginners," an essay explaining how and why the poetry academy had systematically excluded Rukeyser. The essay opens by evoking Walt Whitman and ends by bemoaning the reception that Rukeyser has received in contemporary poetry:

> How do we reach her? Most of her work is out of print. Poets speak of her, but she is otherwise barely known— least of all for her biographies, which in their visionary scholarship put to shame the genre as it's practiced today included in a major current college anthology, her poems are preceded by patronizing and ignorant commentary ... Had a man of her class and background put forth this kind of lifers in scholarship and theory along with poetry, would it be so difficult to embrace his achievement, to reach him? We reach her of course, as we reach all poetic resources blocked from us by mindless packaging and spiritless scholarship. We reach her by recognizing our need for her, by going to libraries and taking out volume after volume, by going, finally, the crossroads—of poetry,

politics, science, sexuality--and meeting her there, where
she waits, reaching toward us.[11]

At our twenty-first-century crossroads, we desperately need
her work for context and solace. Perhaps the time has come to
return to the radical tools that Rukeyser and her generation
used to write poetry. She treats the poems in this epic book
as individual documentaries, recreating the pan, dissolve, and
swiftness of a camera.

"Mediterranean" ends with Rukeyser learning that her
lover Otto Boch is now fighting in the Spanish Civil War.
"Love's not a trick of the lights," she wrote, but she returned
home with a sense of purpose far beyond any love poem: "we
believe, we remember, we saw."[12] Below her final lines in the
New Masses is a lithograph from the social realist and muralist
Michael Lenson. It is the image of a freedom fighter lean-
ing on his rifle, his bayonet glittering as the flames from a
burning house illuminate the darkness. His bare biceps are
cut like a Greek Olympian, reminding us that the poet's
whole adventure began with an international sporting event
but ended with her bearing witness to some of the earliest
atrocities of World War II. Rukeyser leaves Otto behind. His
body and his memory are turned mythological by the historic
events unfolding around them. She told his story. She told
their story.

INTERLUDE
Underground Libraries

The New York Public Library created an open-air library in Bryant Park during the Great Depression, stacking two hundred books under a blue and yellow umbrella to create a pop-up literary community in the middle of Depression-era Manhattan. Homeless people mingled with insolvent scholars. Job hunters debated books with businessmen, all of them sitting on park benches, looking for a purpose.

The New York Times captured the scene: "A man with rumpled gray hair, horn-rimmed glasses far down on his nose and a worn belt holding up shiny blue trousers around his ample stomach exchanged literary comments with an immaculately dressed neighbor."[13]

The most popular books of the summer of 1935 were *What the Hell Are You Living For* by the psychologist Joseph L. Greenbaum and *Succeeding With What You Have* by the steel baron Charles M. Schwab. The paper noted: "[W]ith scores of unemployed persons sunning themselves in the park between rounds of job seeking, it soon became evident that the supply of economic writings was inadequate."[14]

By 1936, there were 600 books and 39,825 check-outs. Only 34 books were stolen over the course of the summer. By 1937, the outdoor library tracked 72,000 check-outs.

How much is a book worth today? How much is a book worth after sitting forgotten on a library shelf for seventy years? These questions of a writer's value initiated and then stalled the most ambitious digital library project in history, the Google Books Library Project.

The controversial Google Books project began in December 2004. The company scanned millions of books from libraries at Harvard, Stanford, the University of Michigan, and the University of Oxford, hoping to make these books available to readers online, to "increase the visibility of in and out of print books, and generate book sales via 'Buy this Book' links and advertising."[15]

Unfortunately, they scanned these books without asking for permission from the copyright holders. I prefer to think that they hoped to preserve lost books by writers like Maxwell Bodenheim or Edward Newhouse. However, the Authors Guild promptly sued Google, reaching a historic, but temporary settlement in 2009. A federal judge tentatively approved a $125 million settlement between Google and the Authors Guild, stipulating that Google would spend $34.5 million to build a Rights Registry to analyze the scanned books. Forty-five million dollars from the settlement would go to pay authors and publishers for works that were still in copyright—paying authors between $60 and $300 for each book scanned by the company.

The Authors Guild walked a thin line: while tasked with fighting for writers' paychecks, they also realized that no one else would ever have the resources to mount such a massive digitization effort. Even the microfiche records I explored at libraries are decaying. Millions more books could crumble into dust while we wait for publishers, authors, or the government to decide what to do with them.

In 2011, the U.S. Circuit Court Judge Denny Chin rejected the $125 million settlement negotiated between the Authors Guild, the Association of American Publishers, and Google. The judge wrote:

> While the digitization of books and the creation of a universal digital library would benefit many, the [settlement] would simply go too far . . . Indeed, the [amended settlement] would give Google a significant advantage over competitors, rewarding it for engaging in wholesale copying of copyrighted works without permission, while releasing claims well beyond those presented in the case.[16]

In October 2012, the publishers involved in the lawsuit reached a settlement with Google. While the exact terms were not disclosed, the new agreement allowed publishers to choose whether or not to sell books that have been digitized by the Google Library Project in the Google Play marketplace. One year later, Judge Chin then dismissed the Authors Guild suit against Google for violating copyright. He defended Google's digitization project, saying that: "It advances the progress of the arts and sciences, while maintaining respectful consideration for the rights of authors and other creative individuals, and without adversely impacting the rights of copyright holders . . . Indeed, all society benefits."[17]

During this period, Google and Amazon engaged in a related struggle over digital book sales. I am a devoted reader of digital books, a marketplace that has been singlehandedly created by Amazon. In his first official statement of 2013, Amazon CEO Jeff Bezos bragged that eBooks are now a "multi-billion dollar category" that the company conjured out of thin air in five years.

In 2010, Google created a reseller program to help independent stores sell digital books through their websites to challenge Amazon's market dominance. Two years later, Google decided to abandon the initiative. Google's digital publishing product management director Scott Dougall explained that the program had "not gained the traction that we hoped it would, so we have made the difficult decision to discontinue it."[18]

Amazon designed the perfect corporate loop for distributing digital books: a single device, a proprietary format, and the largest collection of titles. Unfortunately, the company's digital device also neutralized independent bookstores' early attempts to share in this new marketplace.

A new world is coming, as relentlessly as Woolrich's steamroller. Writers have already endured major disruptions as a result of the shift to digital production, but now publishers are feeling the same creeping panic. As eBook sales grow, extremely cheap digital books are slashing the profit margins for publishers.

This became clear in early 2011, when HarperCollins revealed a controversial new library lending policy for eBooks. The company decided that a library could only rent a book twenty-six times before the license would expire. On HarperCollins "Library Love Fest" blog, President of Sales Josh Marwell explained the policy:

> We spent many months examining the issues before making this change. We talked to agents and distributors,

had discussions with librarians, and participated in the Library Journal e-book Summit and other conferences. Twenty-six circulations can provide a year of availability for titles with the highest demand, and much longer for other titles and core backlist. If a library decides to repurchase an e-book later in the book's life, the price will be significantly lower as it will be pegged to a paperback price point.[19]

Suddenly, a publisher was trying to reproduce the gradual decay of a print book with a digital file, trying to simulate the point when a library needs to pull a tattered book off the shelf and buy a new one.

The move also spawned a HarperCollins boycott. Angry librarians and readers built a simple webpage—plain text on a blank white background—urging libraries to avoid buying books from the publisher. By 2013, the founders had ended the boycott with a frustrated note to readers: "the boycott didn't work and does not appear likely to succeed in achieving our aims."

Ursula K Le Guin attacked these library prices in her 2014 speech at the National Book Awards: "I see my own publishers, in a silly panic of ignorance and greed, charging public libraries for an e-book six or seven times more than they charge customers."[20]

But the tactic isn't going anywhere. In 2019, *Publishers Weekly* wrote about how publishers like Macmillan and Penguin Random House were re-evaluating library lending policies. The article included a measured prediction: "While it certainly does not appear imminent, it is not inconceivable that some major publishers could one day dramatically limit or even pull the plug entirely on library e-book lending."[21]

In 2008, a consortium of educational institutions and libraries joined the HathiTrust, a massive effort to digitize millions of books. The effort was entangled in the Authors Guild and publisher's lawsuit against Google for digitizing millions of books. The digital library survived these legal challenges, and now readers can use the service to access a scanned copy of Edward Newhouse's masterpiece, *You Can't Sleep Here* online—the book that introduced me to the Crisis Generation of New York City writers in the first place.

Only 42 libraries around the world have a copy of this book and Amazon only has a single copy for sale: $200. As long as the HathiTrust stays online, readers can still find Newhouse's work that has been out of print for decades. This is not a permanent solution to preserving his legacy, but it will ensure that another generation can still read Newhouse's work.

No matter what happens to Google's troubled library and lending debates, most people can agree that these works should be preserved in a digital format. The millions and millions of books in the archives contain our literary history. With some careful work, we could massively increase our online collection of public domain works, helping new generations discover the books lost in the digital sea.

8. NATHANAEL WEST

Remembering Failure

"Things are still very bad in New York and getting worse, so grow a good big garden,"[1] wrote the novelist Nathanael West in February 1933. Unemployment hit 25 percent that year and things didn't improve. In one photo from those lean years, West stands with his hands in his pockets, wearing a snug two-button suit. Trim and strong with a bushy mustache, he looks like a lumberjack version of Charlie Chaplin.

West worked as a hotel clerk at the Sutton Hotel starting at the beginning of the crash, earning $50 a week at his post. He let his penniless friends stay in the empty hotel rooms, including the critic Edmund Wilson, the novelist James T. Farrell, and the pulp fiction master Dashiell Hammett.

West wrote fiction during the night shift while he was supposed to be working. Obsessed with the guests, he also started steaming open their mail, reading their private letters, and collecting sorrowful stories. He channeled all these voices into his masterpiece, a novel called *Miss Lonelyhearts*. It was scheduled to be published in April. It was supposed to be his ticket out of the hotel and out of poverty.

When Dashiell Hammett showed up at the Sutton Hotel in the winter of 1933, he looked like a pickled marshmallow. He was completely broke. In fact, he was fleeing a thousand-dollar hotel bill at the Pierre—having left behind his luggage and typewriter. He pretended to go for a winter stroll and instead sneaked out wearing his entire wardrobe. His hair was already starting to turn distinguished gray. A stripe of white marked his tough-guy lifestyle. In one author photo, he stares at the camera and his old detective eyes are sharpened by his thick eyebrows and his black mustache.

He'd already written *The Maltese Falcon* and several other great private detective stories, but he hadn't published a book in years. He had abandoned his wife and family the year before, and all winter long his wife had begged his publisher for money. Broke and in debt, Hammett went straight from the Pierre to the Sutton Hotel. He knew West would let him stay there until he finished his next novel.

Once settled at the Sutton, Hammett began the most important rewrite of his entire life. The 18,000-word manuscript for *The Thin Man* had tormented Hammett for two years since he sold the idea to Alfred Knopf. As he attacked the manuscript, Hammett fell into his old pulp fiction habits, sometimes working for thirty hours straight.

Hammett was drinking himself to death, and the novel reflects this chosen form of self-destruction. His new detective Nick spends most of his time drinking in bed or brooding on the couch. In fact, the only action scene in the entire book happens in bed. Waking up from a deep dark hangover, Nick beats a gangster senseless.

In the book's most famous passage, Nick's wife asks him, "When you were wrestling with Mimi, didn't you have an erection?" "Oh, a little,"[2] replies the detective, scandalizing readers around the globe. Nick and Hammett were both impotent, trading in their guns for martinis. The title of *The Thin Man* described the novel's killer, the murder victim, and all of America: everybody was starving to death, even best-selling novelists. It would be Hammett's final novel.

Downstairs at the same hotel, West also toiled away, trying to finish *Miss Lonelyhearts*. Biographer Marion Meade wrote about this period in her book, *Lonelyhearts: The Screwball World of Nathanael West and Eileen McKenney*.

West's book focuses on the life of a misanthropic news-paper writer who writes an advice column for a local paper, answering questions posed by heartbroken readers: "all these things were part of the business of dreams. He had learned not to laugh at the advertisements offering to teach writing, cartooning, engineering, to add inches to the biceps and to develop the bust."[3] From newspaper columns to novels to snake oil ads, West realized that people needed crazy dreams. Readers filled churches, starved for hope—but West would vandalize this hope in every single novel.

Horace Liveright's publishing house put out *Miss Lonelyhearts* in April 1933, but they declared bankruptcy a few weeks later. West found himself stranded in the mid-dle of the Great Depression, his book held hostage to this bankruptcy. His escape plan became a jail sentence. Horace Liveright himself sold off his share of the publisher in 1930. When the *New York Times* asked him about the demise of the publishing house that still bore his name, he muttered: "I'm sorry to hear it."[4] He would die in September, struck down by pneumonia at forty-nine years old.

In 2011, W.W. Norton decided to revive the Liveright brand, opening a new Horace Liveright imprint helmed by Robert Weil, understandably avoiding these Depression-era failures in a press release. Contemplating the resurrection of this famous desperate publisher in the midst of another economic collapse, Weil wrote:

> I am thrilled to be able to take the lead in creating a twenty-first-century Liveright. It is immensely gratifying to know that now, in 2011—when so many pundits bemoan the collapse of traditional publishing and speak of a world in which the Internet has ravaged the human attention span—Norton stands ready to move even more strongly in the direction of enduring quality.[5]

The press release mentions many authors: E. E. Cummings, Djuna Barnes, and William Faulkner. It does not mention the failures of the Crisis Generation.

What is the best way to remember failure? D. H. Lawrence considered the question in his introduction to Edward Dahlberg's novel, *Bottom Dogs*:

> When we think of America, and of her huge success, we never realize how many failures have gone, and still go to build up that success. It is not till you live in America, and go a little under the surface, that you begin to see how terrible and brutal is the mass of failure that nourishes the roots of the gigantic tree of dollars.[6]

Liveright's complicated life included a powerful set of failures, but stories like these never end up on our bookshelf of writing handbooks. We shouldn't skim over the failures in our literary canon. We need them now.

"Times When Even Clowns Must Grow Serious"

Nathanael West managed to salvage *Miss Lonelyhearts* and republish it, but his sales flagged. It would be more than fifty years until anyone took his work seriously again. He wouldn't be alive to see it. In a few short months, his life had unraveled.

West quit his job at the Sutton Hotel and moved to a busted farm in upstate New York. While he wrote there, a February blizzard rocked New York City, closing the trains and knocking out the power. The storm ended up killing thirteen people: drivers stuck in cars, city workers stranded in snow drifts, old people slipping on ice or starving to death in unheated rooms.

Hundreds of fire alarm boxes froze solid. Nine inches of snow blanketed Manhattan and sixteen inches buried the outlying corners of the metropolis. In Brooklyn, massive snowdrifts actually sealed off the Rockaway peninsula from the rest of the city: no one could escape until firemen dug out the lonely outpost. The city hired twenty thousand temporary workers to shovel the snow, paying fifty cents an hour to desperate laborers in every borough. Western Union contracted horse-drawn sleighs to navigate the ghostly streets. The snow and sleet covered the trees in thick ice sleeves, creating a "fairyland of white-laced draperies,"[7] according to *The New York Times*.

West holed up in his cabin with a stack of Horatio Alger novels from the nineteenth century, reading rags-to-riches stories about plucky poor kids earning their fortunes in America. Alger rewrote the Book of Job for young Americans, trying to persuade readers that suffering and struggle had meaning: his heroes were tortured and mocked by villains, enduring poverty and terrible jobs to earn the American Dream. All his plucky heroes ended up wealthy and respected.

Alger's dreamy prose infuriated West. "Alger is to the American what Homer was to the Greeks,"[8] he wrote. Alger's myths were dangerous in a world where collective action was still a radical—and often illegal—act. West decided to turn Alger's tales into dark parody. In his novel *A Cool Million*, West channeled three years' worth of anger into the fictional adventures of a plucky hero named Lem. Lem goes through all the same trials as Alger's heroes, but every single adventure ends in meaningless ultraviolence. West mutilated Lem like a horror movie character—shredding his leg in a bear trap, chopping off his hand, and scalping him.

While writing the novel, West plagiarized 20 percent of his book from Alger novels, lifting whole paragraphs, cutting them out like letters in a ransom note. In his cabin, West signed all his letters "Ottsville," pretending he lived in the same town as his fictional hero. Lem faces cartoonish levels of misfortune, but West doesn't end the book by granting his cosmic victim a loving chat with God, such as the explanation for misery that Job receives. Instead, the novel ends with pointless murder. "I am a clown . . . but there are times when even clowns must grow serious,"[9] says Lem. And then he is struck down by a sniper's bullet.

Inciting Moments

In 1935, Nathanael West and other novelists marched alongside department store workers who were fighting for a living wage. The protests tied up traffic in the middle of Fourteenth Street outside Ohrbach's department store. Suddenly, protests had broadened to include a whole range of professions. In a Federal Writers Project interview, Irving Fajans, the organizer of the march, recalled a crazy and brave stunt that helped the protestors win their fight:

> There was a dinner being held for Mr. Ohrbach at the Hotel Astor, at which he spoke. Now Ohrbach is supposed to be a big philanthropist, contributes to a lot of charities and such. Well, when he was spouting about some of these public charity funds, two girls who had crashed the dinner by coming in borrowed evening gowns, climbed up on the balcony and chained themselves to the railing. Nobody had noticed them, and suddenly they began shouting in the middle of Ohrbach's speech: 'Charity begins at home! Give your employees shorter hours and better pay!' Of course, there was a big hubbub, and the girls were arrested. But the papers carried a big story, and the boss had to grant our demands to appease public opinion.[10]

Occupy Wall Street had its own inciting moment on Saturday, September 24, 2011, when protests surged up Broadway, headed toward Union Square. "All day, all week, occupy Wall Street," protestors yelled, confounding the police and snarling traffic. The police closed off all the intersections near the park, preparing for arrests.

Eighty activists went to jail that night, but videotaped footage of their arrests surfaced almost instantly. In one such video, we see cops wrapping orange netting around a group of confused women. The two women start screaming, dropping to their knees in the middle of the street. The video went viral, garnering millions of views.

With amplifiers forbidden on park property, the activists used a call-and-response system, echoing speech fragments so the whole crowd could hear. The poet Eileen Myles wrote a goofy poem, playing with the possibilities of a human microphone:

NO I'M THE POET
NO YOU'RE THE POET

NO HE'S THE POET
NO THEY'RE THE POET[11]

A crazed conjugation lesson turns into an affirmation of the art of hundreds of people working in one space for one cause, a living poem about how the Occupy movement could be transmitted to others.

That transmission could be seen best through a flood of "99%" posts made online throughout the Occupy Wall Street protests. When the Occupy Wall Street movement first seized control of Zuccotti Park, news reports mocked them for two weeks, wondering what kind of goals this intentionally leaderless group could possibly have. But America itself was floundering for a focus. No single person could understand what had happened to our country. An entire generation was quietly and bitterly suffering through the recession.

Thousands of Americans ended their silence on the "We Are the 99%" blog. A young father with a few scattered piercings peeked out behind his sheet of paper with a confession. He said he had $150,000 in student loan debt, three children, and no job:

> My Wife, Myself, & my Brother all live together barely scraping by. I can't even go out to look for work due to childcare cost rising so much, any assistance that may have been there before has been cut down and won't allow for anyone else to sign up for it. Waiting list for section 8 is 9 years long. No one in our home is on health insurance except for the kids, god forbid if one of us is actually hospitalized we will all be totally and utterly screwed. Not to mention what happens when Medicaid for children is cut. No heat in the house for this winter, luckily found a space heater down the road from us to heat the kids' room.[12]

"We Are the 99%" In November 2011, protestors march near City Hall in New York City. Photo courtesy Wikimedia Commons.

A veteran with glasses, stubble, and a government buzz-cut also held up a sign:

> I am a 27-year-old veteran of the Iraq War. I enlisted to protect the American people, but ended up making profits for politically-connected contractors. I returned to a country whose economy had been devastated by bankers with the same connections and the same lack of ethics. It might be cliché by now, but this is the second time I've fought for my country and the first time I've known my enemy. I am the 99%."[13]

One family posted a photograph of a bewildered-looking baby beside a neatly-typed sheet of paper that said: "I am 30 days old and I have incurred thousands of dollars of medical debt even though I have good insurance. My mom will still be paying her student loans when I am in college."

Nearly ten people posted every hour for weeks straight. It was a place where everyone could release their frustration at once, sharing the stories that nobody wanted to hear until that exact moment when a couple hundred protestors seized a park in New York City. There was no focus because America had no focus. There was a precedent for this feeling: this chorus of angry and confused voices sounded to me like Fearing's early work, another doomed writer nearly lost forever to obscurity because he wrote the truth about the decade that we all wanted like hell to forget.

The Occupy activists started the Occupy Wall Street Poetry Anthology, a spiritual cousin to the Raven Poetry Circle Anthology. The Occupy Wall Street library printed the Occupy Wall Street Poetry Anthology in a massive binder at the makeshift campgrounds, collecting poems from around the world in a "massive text of dissidence, a testament to the infinite beauty of the human spirit."[14]

The cover was a Molly Crabapple inkpen drawing of a woman typing poetry on her laptop. She glances sideways at the reader. Her pink hair is rumpled and there is a pink sticker pasted on the laptop: MAKE OUT NOT WAR. As the poetry collection circulated both online and offline, it even earned a small story in *The Wall Street Journal*. The poetry collection had major talents like Adrienne Rich, Michael McClure, and Eileen Myles side by side with punk rock poems like "Fuck Capitalism," "Fuck You, Ayn Rand," and "Pledge of Aggrievance." Rock star Patti Smith donated ten copies of her *Just Kids* memoir to the library. She also spent time reading the anthology inside the library.

The anthology opens with "Taking Brooklyn Bridge" by a poet named Stuart. It is a ragged ode to Walt Whitman, containing breathless verses that were composed after Occupy activists brought more than one thousand marchers to Brooklyn Bridge on October 1:

> There was a silent book on the shelf, your book,
> Walt Whitman, I had kept the exact same copy
> I discovered as a youth, inert on the shelf, the song
> You taught me muted in the dark, and I was the same
> As that book, a song stifled in closed pages,
> Serving no one, a dusty decoration.[15]

By November 2011, many cities were looking for ways to evict the Occupy Wall Street protestors, and police clashes grew more frequent around the country. The poet Terence Degnan summed up the mix of revolution and violence in his poem, "Love is a canister of gas you can throw." He wrote about battling cops. He was conflicted because they too were part of the 99 percent. He wrote:

love is the second of hesitation

before the fistfight

and the fistfight itself

love is begging the white collared cops

to lay down their arms

and raise their fists

so that we may fight

as brothers have[16]

In a blog post, the Occupy Wall Street librarians explained why the anthology mattered:

Poetry illuminates the soul of Occupy Wall St. A lot of people are asking, 'What are the demands' and the poets voices show just how nuanced the human spirit and impossible a set of demands truly is. This occupation is about transforming consciousness and the poetry community is a major part of that process.[17]

Occupy Wall Street never found its footing during the first decade of the 2000s, more of this kind of headline-grabbing, street-level action is needed—along with the stories and poems that it inspires. During the Great Depression, journalists, poets, and novelists in New York City marched alongside workers of all kinds. They choreographed demonstrations and they demanded that the world listen. The writers in the 1930s forced newspapers to pay a living wage, pushed publishers to establish more humane working conditions, rewrote the way books were sold in department stores, and convinced the government to create a federal bailout that put thousands of writers around the country back to work.

INTERLUDE
Credit as Storytelling

In October 2007, a full year before the stock market crash nearly destroyed Citibank, the massive conglomerate launched a "Tell Your Story" campaign on television, radio, and the Internet to promote the use of Citi Card credit cards. As the global economy trembled like a set of Jenga blocks supported by reckless credit, the bank described credit card use with cotton-candy language in its press release: "The US Cards advertisements make strong use of Citi's symbolic red arc, a visual metaphor for connecting human aspirations to realities. Both TV and print ads illustrate how Citi Cards enable people to create the stories of their lives by providing the financial power to fund life experiences."[18]

Publicis New York conceived the new campaign, which was an unvarnished attempt to "connect consumers and Citi Cards on an emotional level." Publicis president Rob Feakins explained, as the housing market spiraled out of control and credit card debt mounted to historic levels in those heady days before the crash: "If you think about it, your credit card statement tells a story about the experiences in your life. So, the campaign asks the dangerous question: 'What's your story?

Citibank can help you write it' and aims to communicate that a Citi Card is integral to the answer."[19]

I noticed the ads everywhere, but they seemed innocuous in a city plastered with advertisements on every available space, such as bus stops, telephone poles, and the sides of buildings. Slowly, however, I became obsessed with the ads. When I read that description, I shivered. He actually used the word "dangerous." The quote intended "dangerous" to mean edgy and inspiring, but the more important connotations hovered like ghosts. Dangerous can mean many things, including reckless and ill-conceived. It is a warning, big black letters on a yellow caution sign posted on the edge of a cliff or beside the shark tank.

The ads treated accumulating debt as an art form recasting our rampant borrowing as personal expression. While magazines, newspapers, publisher, and writers struggled to cope with the Great Recession, suddenly everybody with a credit card could be a storyteller. The American Dream seemed like a sick fantasy when retold through these glossy commercials. We all tried to be storytellers with debt, spending our way through stores, travel, and new houses while wages stagnated and unemployment soared.

But the banks were the only institutions with a safety net. One year after the "What's Your Story?" campaign debuted, Citibank teetered on the edge of insolvency, channeling our perverted impulses to use credit on a massive scale by betting on toxic mortgages. Michael Lewis outlined the scope of the disaster in *The Big Short*. He described Citibank's federal bailout at the height of the stock market crash:

> Just weeks after receiving its first $25 billion taxpayer investment, Citigroup returned to the Treasury to

confess that—lo!—the markets still didn't trust
Citigroup to survive. In response, on November 24, the
Treasury granted another $20 billion from TARP and
simply guaranteed $306 billion of Citigroup's assets.
Treasury didn't ask for a piece of the action, or management changes, or for that matter anything at all
except for a teaspoon of out-of-the-money warrants
and preferred stock. The money warrants and preferred
stock. The $306 billion guarantee—nearly 2 percent of
U.S. gross domestic product, and roughly the combined
budgets of the departments of Agriculture, Education,
Energy, Homeland Security, Housing and Urban
Development, and Transportation--was presented
undisguised, as a gift.[20]

Amazingly, even after this corporate catastrophe, Citibank
didn't change its marketing plan one bit. They continued to
pour money into the innocuous "What's Your Story?" campaign. Instead of just using the campaign to represent Citi
Card business, they expand the ads to cover all parts of
Citibank business. The ad campaign won an Effie Award in
2009, reflecting that Citi Card usage increased by 8.4 percent
in the middle of the Great Recession while these ads ran.

In December 2011, the subway tunnels were plastered
with posters for the expanded campaign. The bank promoted
checking accounts, home mortgage services, and shopping
credit cards, all using the same storytelling-driven campaign.
While wandering those crowded tunnels, and seeing every
expensive inch of the walls covered in these slick posters, you
could imagine nearly every aspect of your life connected to
this bank through monster squid tentacles seething behind
the shiny posters.

In 2011, Citibank sold my consolidated student loan debt to
Sallie Mae, which was part of a larger marketplace for trading

student loan debt, and yet another set of poisonous assets poised for a global meltdown as a generation of students confronted epic unemployment after accumulating massive debt for college. The money I invested in a reading and writing education became pocket change in a global marketplace for the futures of American students. A fraction of that money was skimmed off the top of these terrible exchanges to pay for an advertising campaign that sugarcoated a disastrous recession, a shady bank bailout, and the future of a generation shackled to virtual serfdom over student loans.

"What's Your Story?" they asked us, perverting a ruined profession and distorting the very words we used to describe our own experiences. At the height of the Great Depression, Franklin Roosevelt chastised our entire nation for abusing credit and mounted a massive national bailout that put everybody— from farmers to construction workers to clerks to writers—back to work. We bailed out the banks and left everybody else to fend for themselves. And the banks continued to urge us to tell stories by spending imaginary money, asking us "What's Your Story?" on shiny posters plastered around the country, coating our national disaster in a sticky glaze.

We've recovered but we are still sick. We are alienated from our own labor and our daily economic realities are completely separated from our true spending power. The sick and twisted logic of credit that produced our recession is celebrated in award-winning campaigns; we are urged to spend beyond our means and tell our story about it, a very literal kind of false hope, the kind of false hope that will end up sinking our country again.

9. RICHARD WRIGHT

The Popular Front

In the summer of 1935, a young novelist named Richard Wright hitchhiked from Chicago to be a part of the first annual American Writer's Congress in New York City. The conference was sponsored by the *New Masses*. At the conference, Wright mingled with Edward Newhouse, Maxwell Bodenheim, and all the other leaders of the radical literary world.

The Writers Congress had been called to mobilize writers for the "Popular Front." The Communist Party had decided to abandon its formerly antagonistic stance against American liberals in an attempt to move radical politics into the lives of everyday Americans. The precedent had been set in France, where Communist Party members worked together with unions to mount a national strike in the mid-1930s. The party was moving away from enforcing hardline ideology toward a broader, more accepting platform.

The literary scholar Walter Rideout described the new spirit: "it called politically for cooperation with President Roosevelt's New Deal; it called ideologically for an alliance with capitalist democracy; it called 'culturally' for a joining of hands with those who wrote social reform, even if that, rather than of social revolution."[1] During the conference, the League of American Writers was created, writers uniting around a platform that was every bit as radical and wide-ranging as the Sunrise Movement's resolution:

> . . . fight against imperialist war and fascism; for the development and strengthening of the revolutionary labor movement; against white chauvinism (against all forms of Negro discrimination or persecution) and against persecution of minority groups and of the foreign born; solidarity with colonial people in their struggles for freedom; against bourgeois distortions in American literature, and for the freedom of imprisoned writers and artists, and all other class-war prisoners throughout the world.[2]

The Communist Party swelled in the United States during this brief period of unification. The party counted 30,000 members in 1935, but the ranks exploded to a peak of 80,000 members by 1938. It was the last moment in American history where "communist" might still hold positive connotations. At the height of this radical readjustment, the circulation of the *New Masses* surged past 100,000 copies in the winter of 1936, the peak print run of its entire lifetime as a magazine. It was then that the magazine published one of Richard Wright's first poems:

> I am black and I have seen black hands, millions and millions of them
>
> They were tired and awkward and calloused and grimy and covered with hangnails,
>
> And they were caught in the fast-moving belts of machines and snagged and smashed and crushed, And they jerked up and down at the throbbing machines massing taller and taller the heaps of gold in the banks of bosses.[3]

New Masses editor Joseph North recalled reading the poem for the first time: "I admit it: I did not think the first poem of an unknown, young Negro writer we published was, say, the equal of Langston Hughes' work or Carl Sandburg's or Robert Frost's ... we published it hoping to encourage whoever he was . . . Did we catch the essence of the time? Yes, I think we did. It is in our pages, brighter than it is on the paper of any other journal of that time."[4]

For a brief period during the 1930s, politics and writing were entwined in previously unimaginable ways. Writers were organized in vast numbers, writers joined picket lines, and Communist leaders fed money to these young journals. The *New Masses* described the revolutionary spirit that inspired the writers at the conference:

> The capitalist system crumbles so rapidly before our eyes that, whereas ten years ago scarcely more than a handful of writers were sufficiently far-sighted and courageous to take a stand for proletarian revolution, today hundreds of poets, novelists, dramatists, critics, short story writers and journalists recognize the necessity of personally helping to accelerate the destruction of capitalism and the establishment of a workers' government ... Many revolutionary writers live virtually in isolation, lacking opportunities to discuss vital problems with their fellows. Others are so absorbed in the revolutionary cause that they have few opportunities for thorough examination and analysis. Never have the writers of the nation come together for fundamental discussion.[5]

Even now, with a more multicultural literary scene, the *New Masses'* most radical ideas seem almost impossible for twenty-first-century writers to imagine. Could millions of Americans rise up in an economic revolt? The idea that our culture could produce a "workers' government" seems foreign to all of us. As the Soviet Union eroded during the Cold War, the direct connection between writers and Communism was practically severed in the United States. But politics aside, this ideological shift produced a much deeper and lasting effect on writers.

Depression-era writers could hardly imagine the computer-generated isolation that twenty-first-century writers face. Contemporary writers are a scattered bunch. We huddle over computer screens and smartphones. We tweet; we post on Facebook; we blog without pay. An old headline from *The Onion* reads "Novelists Strike Fails To Affect Nation Whatsoever," mocking the idea that writers could ever take collective action that would be noticed. The novelists in the satirical piece called for: "an immediate halt to all new novels, novellas, and novelettes from coast to coast."[6] Nevertheless, the imaginary strike doesn't work: "Bookstores across the country saw no measurable change in anything. Nor has America's economy seen any adverse effects whatsoever, as consumers easily adjust to the sudden cessation of any bold new sprawling works of fiction or taut psychological character studies."[7]

The saddest part of the article is that twenty-first-century Americans find it inconceivable and laughable that novelists would ever organize, or that they have any sort of leverage as cultural workers. As the satirical *Onion* article proved, the idea of novelists mounting collective action in the twenty-first century is literally a joke. Writers have been surgically separated from the working class.

"You Stand on the Borderline"

Wright returned to Chicago after the conference, but he longed to be a part of the New York City literary scene. Chicago had incubated his talent, but New York would make him famous. In 1934, the young writer stumbled into his first John Reed Club, seeking a new kind of literary community. Named after the famous American Communist and journalist, these clubs sprang up all around the country in the 1930s, giving creative people a place to talk about radical ideals.

Reed was the author of *Ten Days That Shook the World*, a famous American memoir about the Russian revolution. Following highly public trials over his connections to Russia, Reed spent his final days in the Soviet Union, dying of typhus in 1920. These clubs formed in his honor published pamphlets and magazines around the country, hosting lectures and rallies to inspire Americans to join the Communist cause.

Wright described the first time he climbed the stairs to a club meeting, wandering past shadowy murals of revolutionary events. "What on earth could take place in such a dingy room? ... I opened [the door] and stepped onto the strangest room I had ever seen. Paper and cigarette butts lay on the floor."

Wright found an instant community:

> A Jewish boy who was to become one of the nation's leading painters, to a chap who was to become one of the eminent composers of his day, to a writer who was to create some of the best novels of his day, to a young Jewish boy who was destined to film the Nazi occupation of Czechoslovakia. I was meeting men and women who were to form the first sustained relationships of my life.[8]

Throughout the 1930s, these radicals gave Wright the leverage he needed to survive the punishing economy, helping him hone his craft. A few months after his New York trip, the *New Masses* assigned him his first news story. Wright wrote a bombastic account of his Chicago neighborhood's reaction to a legendary boxing match between Joe Louis and Max Baer, exploring the power of these millions of African Americans, a power that could be channeled either into violence or organized action.

He wrote:

> You stand on the borderline wondering what's beyond. Then you take one step and you feel a strange, sweet tingling. You take two steps and the feeling becomes keener. You want to feel some more. You break into a run. You know it's dangerous, but you're impelled in spite of yourself. Four centuries of oppression, of frustrated hopes, of black bitterness, felt even in the bones of the bewildered young, were rising to the surface. Yes, unconsciously they had imputed to the brawny image of Joe Louis all the balked dreams of revenge, all the secretly visualized moments of retaliation, AND HE HAD WON! Good Gawd Almighty! Yes, by Jesus, it could be done! Didn't Joe do it? You see, Joe was the consciously felt symbol. Joe was the concentrated essence of black triumph over white. And it comes so seldom, so seldom. And what could be sweeter than long nourished hate vicariously gratified? From the symbol of Joe's strength they took strength, and in that moment all fear, all obstacles were wiped out, drowned. They stepped out of the mire of hesitation and irresolution and were free! Invincible! A merciless victor over a fallen foe! Yes, they had felt all that-for a moment . . .[9]

The *New Masses* didn't pay Richard Wright for the Joe Louis story. According to Hazel Rowley's biography, Wright wouldn't earn a dime for his writing until 1936 when he was the only African American published in the writing anthology *The New Caravan*.

***

Throughout the first decade of the 2000s, moments of protest have brought us to the brink of something new, but we have always pulled back. Occupy Wall Street met a quick, forceful end in 2011, and all that energy never pushed us into the beyond.

Through digital cameras live-streaming online, I watched the police dismantle Occupy Wall Street the morning of November 15, 2011, a few days short of the movement's three-month anniversary.

Everybody was getting ready to go to sleep when the police showed up with eviction notices. The protestors huddled around the kitchen tarp, singing and chanting slogans. On the livestream broadcast, the cops looked sheepish, striking odd poses as they gradually outnumbered the last activists huddled in the corner.

A massive dump truck arrived, parking at the corner where the police tossed tents, tarps, blankets, and hundreds of donated supplies. Tents fluttered in the air. The last group of protestors moved to the back of the park, chanting, banging drums. They yelled at the cops, framed by an American flag.

Police spotlights lit the park, making it as bright as a movie set. The protestors sang Woody Guthrie songs while the city dismantled the camp. The cops wore plastic visors and helmets, bracing for madness. The cops surrounded the last demonstrators in a tight formation.

A cameraman interviewed the last remaining activists. They were scared but stubborn. One protestor was chained to a pole:

> Scared as hell but I'm not moving
>
> I hope this doesn't turn into another Oakland
>
> This is not the end

I kept hitting refresh on my computer, but the livestream crapped out as the line of riot cops thickened. I followed the last few seconds of the raid on Twitter through reports from *Mother Jones'* Josh Harkinson. His old tweets read like a brief poem:

> The riot police moved in with zip cuffs and teargassed the occupiers in the food tent
>
> Then they wrestled them to the ground and cuffed them
>
> Everyone I witnessed being arrested was resisting peacefully
>
> He said that all the press is in the press pen, and that's where I had to go.[10]

That was the end of Occupy Wall Street.

For the next few months, I wrote about the fate of Occupy Wall Street and the related court cases that sprung up as a result, but I watched reader interest in the story taper off in Google Analytics, which became a real-time map of how public opinion waned. Writers returned to pre-1930 conditions: unorganized, broke, and easily manipulated.

Portrait of Harlem

After his Joe Louis essay, Wright began polishing a collection of four novellas called *Uncle Tom's Children*. The book explores both the promise of organization and the violent implications of actual strikes. It ends with "Fire and Cloud," a novella about an African American preacher brutally horse-whipped for supporting his community members in a union march. While Wright described the beating with graphic and biblical imagery, he reconciled the violence with a triumphant march through the center of the preacher's small town, a massive crowd building around economic interests instead of hateful racial ideas: "When they reached the park that separated the white district from the black, the poor whites were waiting. Taylor trembled when he saw them join, swelling the mass that moved toward the town. He looked ahead and saw black and white marching; he looked behind and saw black and white marching."[11]

Wright returned to New York City in June 1937 for the second biannual American Writers Congress. The radical conference opened with a speech by Ernest Hemingway about his time in Spain during the bloodiest days of the Spanish Civil War. The war had become a major cause for radicals around the world, and was an early test of Popular Front politics on a global scale. Along with a number of American writers and intellectuals, Hemingway fought against Franco's armies. In his speech entitled "Fascism Is a Lie," he launched an explosive attack on Franco's rule in Spain and the economic problems facing writers around the world:

> Because of the difficulty of making true, lasting writing, a really good writer is always sure of eventual recognition. Only romantics think that there are such thugs as unknown masters. Really good writers are always rewarded under almost any existing system of government that they can tolerate. There is only one form of government that cannot produce good writers, and that system is fascism. For fascism is a lie told by bullies. A writer who will not lie cannot live or work under fascism.[12]

Wright's support for Communism peaked in 1938, when the author joined Langston Hughes, Nelson Algren, and other writers in signing a petition in support of Joseph Stalin. Many of these writers (including Wright) would eventually denounce Stalin's murderous reign in his own country.

After this Congress, Wright decided to move to New York City for good. He headed east later that year, jobless in the middle of a punishing Depression. Wright found a place to sleep in Harlem, using a friend's apartment downtown for an office. It was a major career risk. He waited anxiously for a transfer to the New York City FWP.

In the meantime, Wright took a job as a reporter at *The Daily Worker*. As the Harlem correspondent for the Communist rag, he earned $80 a month—$45 less than he earned in Chicago. According to the biographer Hazel Rowley, *The Daily Worker* was the only newspaper in the country that actually paid African American reporters.

In November 1937, he wrote a letter to the novelist Ralph Ellison, describing the hectic pace of his newspaper job: "I am working from 9 a.m. to 9 and 10 p.m. and it's a hard, hard grind. Can't do any work, haven't the time. I am thinking definitely in terms of leaving here, but I don't know when. I seem to be turning my life into newspaper copy from day to day; and when I look to the future it looks no better."[13]

The prevailing myth—then as now—was that writers needed to suffer. At the height of the Great Depression, the newspaper columnist Elise Robinson published a column about writers in her syndicated column:

> No writer is worth shucks until he can take and has taken punishment. ... He's supposed to go hungry and ragged and cold, to drudge at chores he loathes, to suffer endless

> humiliation and rejection doing the thing he loves in
> infrequent, stolen moments or bakes beans. It MAKES
> a writer, and weeds out the POSEURS, the people with
> a smattering of talent but no salt or spunk, lacking which
> no writer is worth a hoot.[14]

But Wright could barely hold his career together earning peanuts as an overworked newspaper reporter, and he was struggling to do anything creative. If society hadn't built a safety net for writers like him in the guise of the Federal Writers Project, his career would have ended.

According to historian David A. Taylor's history of the Federal Writers Project, Wright got transfer approval and joined the New York City FWP one month later. The same momentous day, Wright won the Story Prize for *Uncle Tom's Children*. The prize earned him $500 and a publishing contract with Harper & Brothers for the unpublished manuscript. They would publish his first book in 1938.

Arguably, these serendipitous moments saved the young writer from oblivion. Contemporary writers have none of the federal support that Wright's generation had; who knows how many young artists have been lost without this federal financial support?

At the FWP in New York City, Wright assumed control of the project's Harlem work. He took over for the scholar and poet Claude McKay. Their work together still stands in their essay "Portrait of Harlem." The essay outlines the literary movements, theaters, bands, and community centers that flourished in the neighborhood. While Wright argues that the creative boom of the Harlem Renaissance "disintegrated" during the Depression, the essay also includes a kinetic

"He's supposed to go hungry and ragged and cold." A salesman peddles hair tonic on Thirty-Eighth Street in November 1936. Photograph by Russell Lee, courtesy the Library of Congress.

section about Harlem dances, cataloging the names and beats of long-forgotten steps:

> Harlem's boast that it is an area where new dance steps are created is indisputable. Just who initiated the "truck" is not known. Cora La Redd of the Cotton Club, "Rubber Legs" Williams, Chuck Robinson, and Bilo and Ashes have all put forward their individual claims. It is interesting to note that there are many kinds of "trucking,"— the "picket's truck," the "politician's truck," the "Park Avenue truck," the "Mae West truck," and the "Hitler truck." Among other contemporary Harlem dances is the "shim-sham," a time-step featuring the "break" with a momentary pause; and the "razzle-dazzle," which involves a rhythmic clapping of hands and a rolling of hips. The riotous "Lindy Hop" is a flying dance done by couples in which a girl is thrown away in the midst of a lightning two-step, then rudely snatched back to be subjected to a series of twists, jerks, dips, and scrambles. All of these and many more can be seen in Harlem's dance halls, at house parties, on beaches, and in the streets in summer to the tune of WPA Music Project bands.[15]

Wright repeatedly ties these artistic breakthroughs to organized labor. He cites the music industry's budding unionization movement at the climax of the essay:

> Most of the prominent Negro bands have reached a large public through their phonograph recordings, and Negro band-members are protected by the powerful Local 802 of the American Federation of Musicians, affiliated with the American Federation of Labor—though there are evidences of discrimination against Negroes in the matter of wages.

"Portrait of Harlem" is packed with telling details about the civil rights struggle of the day, a record of how regular New Yorkers fought for basic services. This all happened an entire generation before the Freedom Riders and Martin Luther

King Jr. rode buses around the country. Wright calls Harlem during the Great Depression the "focal point in the struggle for the liberation of the Negro people."

In one passage, he captures how even a movie theater became a battleground as Harlem residents expressed solidarity with Africans around the world in confronting the poisonous transmission of fascism:

> During Italy's invasion of Ethiopia, anything concerning Italy on the movie screen brought forth immediate hisses and catcalls. In the consciousness of this oppressed community, current events are commonly interpreted as gains or set-backs for the Negro people. This social restlessness results in many public demonstrations. Harlemites in increasing numbers attend street meetings protesting evictions; picket stores to compel the hiring of Negroes, or WPA offices to indicate disapproval of cuts in pay or personnel; parade against the subjection of colonial peoples, or to celebrate some new civic improvement; and march many miles in May Day demonstrations.[16]

These brave activists laid the foundation for our civil rights movement, and they deserve better than a few pages locked away in a forgotten guidebook. As a Communist and an African American, Wright was trapped between two related but divergent causes: racial and economic equality. His passage about a fiery riot in his neighborhood encapsulated the entire conflict:

> The most serious rioting that Harlem has known occurred in the spring of 1935, at a time when many of the white-owned business establishments on West 125th Street were being boycotted for their refusal to employ Negroes. A leading figure in the attendant agitation was a person calling himself Sufi Abdul Hamid, who in gaudy Egyptian uniform preached anti-Semitism on the street corners and was regarded by Harlem's Jewish merchants as a "Black

Hitler." On March 19 a Negro boy was caught stealing in one of the boycotted stores. Rumors immediately spread throughout Harlem that the boy had been beaten and killed by the white proprietor; large crowds gathered in and near West 125th Street, and in spite of police efforts an orgy of window-smashing and store-looting followed. As emphasized in the report of an investigating committee appointed by Mayor La Guardia, the outbreak had its fundamental causes in the terrible economic and social conditions prevailing in Harlem at the time.[17]

A New Book of Job

Even during this period of government-sponsored writing work, Wright and his fellow writers faced the constant threat of elimination. One round of summer layoffs spawned another week of massive protests. FWP workers marched in protests alongside Communists and other writers. Author Harry Roskolenko described the motley crew on the picket lines: "furriers and garment workers, Bowery bums and Broadway actresses, in proletarian loyalty, joined the picket lines of our literary ranks."[18]

According to Roskolenko, the police shut off the power in the building during these ongoing strikes. He remembered a cozy feeling of solidarity in those mixed up days: "They sat in the officially darkened project building which they relit with red candles. Singing red songs, they established nocturnal dictatorship over the covered typewriters."[19]

Things turned ugly during that week of chaos. Agitators at the protest started stabbing police horses with needles as the cops charged the ranks of writers. A massive riot exploded outside the offices, complete with "busted heads and "shrieking women."

Amid the tumult of the early Spring, Wright scored a major literary coup. The *New Masses* devoted dozens of pages to his "novelette" *Bright and Morning Star* as the keystone in its special Federal Arts Issue, a literary supplement collecting writing by radical young writers.

The story—also collected in *Uncle Tom's Children*—was published by Harper & Brothers that month through the contest Wright won a year earlier. The story swelled the magazine, and the publisher took out a full page ad with Wright's photograph and a ringing endorsement from *New Masses* editor Granville Hicks: "It is not only a fine piece of writing; it is the beginning of a distinguished career."[20] The literary supplement included a note from the editors, urging the continuation of the program that had kept so many *New Masses* contributors afloat during the Great Depression: "The creative writing presented here indicates the high degree of literary talent on the Federal Writers' Project and emphasizes the need for government support of the arts."[21]

Following these graphic protests, the city hired back a number of writers for a mysterious creative writing project. Richard Wright and Maxwell Bodenheim were among the lucky few picked for the plum assignment, where they would be allowed to work from home. According to Monty Noam Penkower, the work-from-home experiment was scrapped in the spring of 1938 because the writers exhibited "too much daydreaming and procrastination."[22]

In this new program, Richard Wright began work on the novel that would change the course of his entire career, *Native Son*. Wright also found the time to write an essay called "The Ethics of Living Jim Crow," a series of chilling anecdotes about growing up in the heavily segregated South. The FWP would publish this essay in *American Stuff*, a hastily assembled collection meant to appease Washington, D.C.'s desire for results from the New York City project. The collection includes work by a mix of prominent FWP writers and stories recorded around the country by FWP workers.

According to the historian Monty Noam Penkower, Wright was the star of the collection despite reservations: "the editors fortunately realize it was 'the no. 1 piece in the book,' despite [the national director's] hesitation over its frank truths."[23] In the essay, Wright explains how he had to forge a note from a white man to check out books at the library: "I never took any chances guessing with the white librarian about what the fictitious white man would want to read. No doubt if any of the white patrons had suspected that some of the volumes they enjoyed had been in the home of a Negro, they would not have tolerated it for an instant."[24]

Wright had confronted economic disaster and survived, partly because this floundering federal project had kept him alive during those rough years. Wright's *Native Son* begins with a blazing epigraph from The Book of Job: "Even today is my complaint rebellious / My stroke is heavier than my groaning."[25] In this passage, Job refuses to bow to the overwhelming misfortune dealt by the Devil, shaking a clenched fist at the sky as he endures his cosmic misfortune. While his gesture proves useless in the end, Job's "heavy stroke" pounds the empty first page of the novel. This new novel tackled the mute frustration of the Depression, the same feeling that he struggled to describe in the *New Masses* poem from 1934. He describes the change that took place before writing *Native*

Son in an essay. He was frustrated by the effect of *Uncle Tom's Children* on the people he was trying to reach:

> I had written a book which even bankers' daughters could read and weep over and feel good about. I swore to myself that if I ever wrote another book, no one would weep over it; that it would be so hard and deep that they would have to face it without the consolation of tears. It was this that made me get to work in dead earnest.[26]

Native Son would blend revolutionary poetry with the rowdy violence of a Joe Louis fight. Wright wrote his first draft in four feverish months. As his colleagues marched and went on strikes, he wrote a novel about a black man named Bigger Thomas who accidentally kills a white woman and then flees into the ghettoes of Chicago. "The first book flowed like a dream,"[27] he said in a later essay.

No literary theory can ever explain the dreamy brutality that punctuates the first section of the novel, ending as Bigger saws off the head of a dead white woman and burns her body in the furnace. Wright described his main character:

> He hated his family because he knew that they were suffering and that he was powerless to help them. He knew that the moment he allowed himself to feel to its fullness how they lived, the shame and misery of their lives, he would be swept out of himself with fear and despair. So he held toward them an attitude of iron reserve; he lived with them, but behind a wall, a curtain.[28]

While Wright was writing his manuscript, a black teenager named Robert Nixon murdered a white woman with a brick during a botched robbery in Chicago. The newspapers pounced on the story, fueling false rumors that the burglar had raped his victim before the murder. Hazel Rowley described the trial: "The white press didn't even pretend to objectivity. Nixon was referred to a 'jungle negro,' a 'Negro rapist,' a 'sex fiend,' a 'moron slayer.' He was repeatedly described as 'ape-like.'"[29]

Wright cut and pasted these racist newspaper headlines straight into his bleak novel, letting an unfortunate piece of American history convict his readers. After a weeklong trial, the white jury gave Nixon the death penalty. He was executed by electric chair a year after the murder.

Before Bigger destroys himself, Wright gives him a fleeting glimpse of the hope and solidarity that Communism could provide. But these hopes are ultimately swept away by bad luck and violence:

> Dimly, he felt that there should be one direction in which he and all other black people could go whole-heartedly; that there should be a way in which gnawing hunger and restless aspiration could be fused; that there should be a manner of acting that caught the mind and body in certainty and faith. But he felt that such would never happen to him and his black people, and he hated them and wanted to wave his hand and blot them out.[30]

Native Son became a controversial bestseller at the end of the Depression. According to literary scholar Walter Rideout, the novel sold 250,000 copies in a couple of months, which are astounding sales for a radical novel. Wright won the Most Distinguished American Novel award at the fourth annual Writers Congress in 1941.

In 2019, the Pulitzer-winning playwright Suzan-Lori Parks reimagined *Native Son* in 2019 Chicago, reviving the novel against our contemporary racial tension, gang violence, and economic inequality. But Wright managed a feat that radical writers like Newhouse and Maxwell Bodenheim could never achieve: he took the plight of the starving masses and converted it into a suspenseful and violent narrative that dragged readers through until the end.

Once again, we find ourselves standing on the borderline.

10. EDWARD NEWHOUSE & THE CRISIS GENERATION

Red Scares

Even though he was the first writer to define the Crisis Generation, Edward Newhouse would eventually renounce his writings from the 1930s. The novelist and journalist began to drift away from the Communist Party while writing his second novel, *This Is Your Day*. The book was published in 1937, right in the middle of one of Stalin's most brutal campaigns against his critics in the Soviet Union. Stalin's three-year-long Moscow Trials climaxed in the exile of Trotsky and mass executions in Russia. "The Moscow trials left me without any political moulds to pour into," Newhouse said in an interview with *Twentieth Century Authors*, "and I had to set about learning how to write of things as they appeared to my own untrained eyes."[1]

This Is Your Day continued the adventures of Gene Marsay, the unemployed newspaper reporter from *You Can't Sleep Here*. Marsay ends up working as a Communist organizer. The book recounts his failed attempts to prevent the foreclosure of 4,000 farms in upstate New York. The novel pivots around a tense court scene where a judge refuses to stop the foreclosures despite Marsay's massive campaign to organize the farmers. The farmers briefly grab weapons, but the organizer stops them before they confront the National Guard troopers outside the courthouse. Bloodshed is averted, but it is a frustrating end.

The book is loaded with unsatisfied desires. Marsay's girl-friend's mother reflects on her strained sex life, detailing the bleak state of Depression-era sex: "He would advance upon her abjectly and with desperate apologies and a maddening, servile, persistent vigor that was impossible to ward off. And on just such a morning-after he was even more abject than usual, and miserable, and ingratiating with guilt."[2]

Newhouse jumps between the thoughts of four anxious characters throughout this failed novel. His book includes some racy content, an attempt to breathe air into a dying genre. But ultimately, the novel doesn't work. It is crushed by the weight of Communist propaganda, earnest postur-ing, and the need for a sharper editor. I asked Newhouse's daughter, Alison Dinsmore, about this change in her father's writing. "When he was a young man, he deeply believed that Communism was the way to go. By the time the war came along, he felt the opposite. He had dumped those ideas. He thought they were embarrassing. He thought that they read as if they were written by a poseur. To be fair to him, he felt that everybody writing at that age was being a poseur."

As Newhouse reckoned with his own misgivings about his radical politics and writings, the Federal Writers Project also faced Congressional scrutiny as World War II loomed. In 1938, FWP member Edwin Banta took the stand at the Federal Courthouse, testifying that forty percent of those employed by the FWP were Communists. Banta opened his testimony by highlighting the fact that his family first arrived in America in 1659, making him a symbolic patriot. He had worked as a reporter for many years, writing for *New York World*, the *New York American*, and as a classified ad writer for *The New York Times*.

He joined the Communist Party soon after he found work at the FWP. He claimed that party leaders made him promise that he would recruit more radicals, incite violence at strikes, and pass a can to collect money for antifascist fighters in Spain. As his most damning piece of evidence, he revealed a handbook called *The People's Front*, detailing the party's push for a more universal and palatable approach. It was inscribed: "presented to Comrade Edwin Banta by the members of the Federal Writers Project and the Communist Party of the USA in recognition of his devotion to untiring efforts in behalf of the party and communism."[3]

A number of other writers signed the book, including Maxwell Bodenheim, who doodled a cartoon hammer and sickle beside his name. Federal critics of the project would use the book as a smoking gun in future hearings. Former FWP supervisor Jerre Mangione had no kind words for the former dues collector:

> Banta, it developed, was not a benign old Communist but a right-wing informer. It was his testimony together with the incriminating book that led Congressman [Martin] Dies to choose the FWP in 1938 as a primary target for attack—an attack that proved to be the beginning of the end for federal sponsorship of all the arts projects.[4]

As this controversy derailed the project, the *New Masses* published a literary supplement that cheered the achievements of the WPA at the end of the Great Depression. "What of this new generation, the literary generation of the depression, the young talents reared to maturity amid economic catastrophe?"[5]

asked the editors of the *New Masses*, in an uncharacteristically hopeful essay about the future of the Federal Writers Project specifically and of the future of American federal government patronage for art generally.

The editors raised the question at the project's darkest moment. The supplement included poems by a number of writers from this book, including a poem by Bodenheim that described a grandmother watching her granddaughter marching with fellow radicals during the Great Depression:

> A young grand-daughter, ribboned and sedate,
>
> Handing out leaflets, marching under banners
>
> Proclaiming "Down with Fascist War and Hate."[6]

Watching her granddaughter, the old woman wishes that she had lived a more radical life. She turns to her husband and sighs, "All that we did was misbehave."

Before the poems, the *New Masses* editors described the "literary drought" of the Great Depression when writers had eked out a living "on the bounties of angels"[7] by publishing in journals and magazines even smaller than the *New Masses* before the FWP. Things began to change when writers scattered around the country "discovered within them a common interest and bond," and started to fight for their place in the New Deal. The editors thought the FWP marked a new era in American culture. The supplement included a full-page Harper & Brothers advertisement for Wright's *Uncle Tom's Children* collection. Below a resolute photograph of Wright, one glowing blurb read: "This man can write. These stories are more than American literature. Their spirit is part of a new American history."[8] Reading those lines in the twenty-first century with Black Lives Matter activists marching against unabated police violence and a resurgence of white nationalism, I wish the "new American history" that blurb predicted had truly come to pass.

The editors of the *New Masses* saw the FWP as a historic shift in American culture. They wrote:

> The trend from individual patronage to public subsidy will be completed. The transition from the eclectic art of coterie's and private enterprise, represented by the little magazines in the egocentric figure of the Bohemian out-cast, to an art of serving the public need and represented by the artist of the Republic will be resolved. The new generation will come of age. The relationship between the American public and its writers whom it subsidizes through governmental agencies will find expression in a people's literature.[9]

That dream would never be realized. When Congress voted to extend the FWP program in 1939, the funds now came with new rules and massive political purges. All workers had to sign affidavits that they were not Communists, and over four hundred workers received dismissal notices by August 1940 because of alleged subversive activities.

Congressman Dies continued to attack the FWP, call-ing it "a deliberate long-time use of government publications to spread class hatred throughout the United States."[10] One of his Congressional witnesses denounced the project as a "school for Communist writers" and another witness claimed that the Communists used the project to obtain intelligence on how to attack or "demoralize" New York City. His work set the stage for Red Scares that would decimate the ranks of American writers a decade later. These allegations and cuts would ultimately unravel the FWP. And, despite a number of economic downturns in the United States, no one has ever managed to replicate the program.

Public subsidy has continued for writers, but these funds are often at the whims of politicians. In 2017, the fates of thousands of struggling writers hung in the balance as politicians bandied proposals to eliminate funding for the National Endowment for the Arts (NEA). Cutting NEA funding will have a severe trickle-down effect on the small press world, as many indie publishers depend on funding from the organization to stay afloat.

The NEA, which had a budget of nearly $148 million in 2016, supports all kinds of artists, but it also helps numerous small publishers throughout the country. In *Publishers Weekly*, I wrote about how those cuts could have impacted Small Press Distribution (SPD), which serves more than 400 small publishers. The money SPD received from the NEA accounted for 4 percent of the nonprofit's $1 million budget. "While 4% may sound like a small percentage of our overall budget, those monies more or less flow through to our hundreds of publishers," Lependorf told me. "A 4% cut to the income of our presses could easily make the difference between just covering costs and just failing to cover their costs. It's the difference between existing or not existing."[11]

In 2015, SPD sold nearly 165,000 books, and its sales exceeded $1.75 million. More than 60 percent of those titles were poetry books—the same kind of literary work being celebrated in the *New Masses* essay. Those fragile voices are just as vulnerable today as they were during the Great Depression.

Newhouse in Los Angeles

Newhouse's break with the Communist Party coincided with a life-altering publication. Toward the end of the Great

Depression, he sold a personal essay to *The New Yorker*, an outlet many pay grades above his radical newspaper work and a million light years away from the ideological stance of those publications. By the end of the Depression, Newhouse had a contract with the magazine. He wrote eighty-one short stories over the course of his life, publishing a staggering fifty stories in *The New Yorker*. The revolutionary had joined the middle class just as the American wartime recovery began.

According to his daughter, Newhouse met his wife in 1939 while riding on a train together. They kept talking for hours and she "cautiously" agreed to see Newhouse again. They were married in 1940. When America entered World War II, Newhouse enlisted in officer's school. Newhouse spent the war writing speeches, handbooks, and memos for the military brass. Newhouse used to tease his daughter, telling her that he would pay her $5 to steal his own books from the library. Now you can't even steal the books. They have been pulped or consigned to rare book websites. Newhouse got his wish for literary obscurity with respect to his early, radical work.

The first thing he ever wrote for *The New Yorker* was an essay about a trip he took to Los Angeles. In the essay, Newhouse recalls his poorest days: living in a YMCA, riding freight cars with hoboes, and sleeping in an "abandoned candy store."[12] While bumming through Los Angeles in the early days of the Depression, the starving writer ended up accidentally linked to Clara Bow, holding the gorgeous actress's arm as she swept to her limo. By the end of the 1930s, Newhouse had finally made good and joined the upper-crust of society for good, leaving behind his stormiest political days. He polished the worst deficiencies in his prose, but he lost the urgency and black humor that used to infuse his best writing.

Edward Newhouse visited Los Angeles a few times during the Great Depression, covering the rise of unions in Hollywood. The movement had begun around 1933, when struggling screenwriters formed the Screen Writers Guild to protest a 50-percent pay cut that rocked the industry. The *New Masses* had Newhouse cover the turmoil, and by the end of the Great Depression, a union culture had taken deep root in the film industry. The Federal Writers Project also published *Los Angeles in the 1930s*, a sunny guidebook to California's legendary city. It included a description of a newly radicalized workforce:

> Hollywood, once so individualistic, became unionized— not only technicians and casual workers, but screen writers, directors, top flight actresses and actors. Celebrities gave up their rounds of social activities and their weekends at Palm Springs to attend and often to lead political forums and meetings, organizing an Anti-Nazi League, the Motion Picture Artists Committee, the Motion Picture Democratic Committee, and, more recently, Associated Film Audiences, designed to marshal public support for artistic films with realistic content and to fight censorship of plays dealing with our current problems.[13]

That Depression-era union infrastructure still stands. Hollywood is one of the only places in America where creators have the same kind of leverage as an industrial worker. Today, the California Film Commission counts nineteen different unions and guilds that steer the movie industry, including the mighty Writers Guild of America West—the contemporary incarnation of the Screen Writers Guild. This powerful group counts thousands of the highest paid writers in the world who all write screenplays under a strict set of Guild guidelines. Indeed, the guidebook makes the metaphor more explicit:

> Los Angeles has become a huge word factory. Fiction, particularly, is turned out on a mass-production scale. Writers from all over the world have been drawn here by the motion pictures and later by the radio studios, as well as by the climate, the natural scene, and the growing cultural activity.[14]

Eighty years later, Los Angeles and its marvelous factory of words managed to be more unionized than radical New York City ever did.

I finished writing this book in Los Angeles, moving here with my wife and two young children a few years ago. Along my daily commute, I pass small homeless encampments. The Hoovervilles that Newhouse explored during the Great Depression did not magically appear out of nowhere. These lonesome communities were built slowly at the margins of every major city. In 2020 Los Angeles, suitcases, junk, and strange sculptures sometimes spill out of the grass along the freeway ramp. The police clear these homeless camps occasionally, but new ones always appear, tucked under overpasses, along access roads, and beside street-level culs-de-sac.

These encampments are symptoms of a disease we don't want to acknowledge. We pretend they aren't there until we can't pretend anymore. We can feel this global economic rot creeping all around us, but things won't change until a writer like Newhouse forces us to see things the way they really are.

CONCLUSION
The Sunrise Movement

We began with Aubrey Williams' plea to *New York Times* readers more than eighty years ago: "Somehow we do have to convince millions of our young people that we have not yet come to a social doomsday, and that there is something better for them to do than jump off the deep end."[1]

Today, a new generation of student activists has already found something better. On college campuses around the country, disparate climate change activists banded together in 2017, creating a new group called the Sunrise Movement. In those early days, Sunrise co-founder Varshini Prakash hosted a Google Hangouts video session with a few hundred other activists. Throughout that digital meeting, members shared their own stories of how climate change had affected their lives and sparked an earnest sense of purpose. These activists understand that they must compel our legislative leaders to act on climate change before scientists' worst projections are realized.

Prakash recounted memories of visiting her grandparents in a region of India hit hard by climate change floods. "I don't think anybody should lose their home, their health, and their families because a small group of wealthy white dudes on the other side of the world are more worried about protecting their profits than the lives of the billions of people who live on this earth,"[2] she said. As the Trump Administration prepared to back out of the Paris Accords in June 2017, these young activists began writing "letters to the future" and burying them in time capsules around the country. They scribbled stories of everything they tried to do to avert the most disastrous climate change scenarios. Prakash explained why they were doing this, laying out the stakes quite plainly: "Climate change is going to define the story of the twenty-first century, a hundred years from now. People alive today are gonna be remembered for what they did or didn't do right now to leave a healthy world for our great grandchildren. This is about who we are and how we will be remembered."[3]

All these activists had were stories. And that was enough to spark a new movement.

The Crisis Generation could hardly have imagined the future where we now live and write. We don't need printing presses to put out poetry anthologies. We have magical smartphones, tablets, and laptops to blast stories into space between cell towers and satellites. Using just a fraction of my device's storage capacity, I can carry digital copies of every single book by every single author I have mentioned so far. And yet, these Great Depression writers are easily forgotten in our daily diet of twenty-first-century content. If we only hold on to one lesson of the Crisis Generation, let's remember this one: they did not surrender.

The Sunrise Movement activists rallied throughout 2018, pushing the idea of a Green New Deal into the center of key Democratic campaigns during the midterm elections. Just before the election, a special United Nations report offered

"We tell our stories and we honor each other's stories." Two Sunrise Movement activists photographed by Charles Edward Miller, courtesy Wikimedia Commons.

the world its "final call" to reverse the worst-case scenarios for global temperature changes. The report called for "rapid, far-reaching and unprecedented changes"[4] before 2030, our final opportunity to keep the temperature shift at 1.5°C. The difference between 1.5°C and 2°C could avert environmental catastrophes that would affect hundreds of millions of people by 2050. The Sunrise Movement took that twelve-year deadline to heart, recirculating that damning figure through protest songs, speeches, and social media.

When the Democrats regained control of the House of Representatives in the midterms, Representative-elect Alexandria Ocasio-Cortez stood beside Sunrise Movement activists in Washington, D.C., flush with success. That December, around 1,000 activists stormed Washington to lobby 50 members of Congress and stage sit-ins at the offices of three key Democratic representatives—incoming House Speaker Nancy Pelosi, Minority Whip Steny Hoyer, and Jim McGovern. Before Congress ended its session for the holidays, 143 Sunrise protestors had been arrested.

The protest paid off, as McGovern pledged to create a select committee to work on the Green New Deal. Just three months later, the Green New Deal resolution counted eighty-nine co-sponsors in the House of Representatives and eleven co-sponsors in the Senate, making climate change an unavoidable issue for the 2020 election.

I have watched the Sunrise Movement grow these last few years, joining local rallies with my 9-year-old daughter. As we stare into the abyss of our own deep end, I place my faith in these young activists. Throughout the COVID-19 crisis, the Sunrise Movement offered free access to "Sunrise

School" online, continuing to mobilize during this dark period with this simple message:

> "Right now, as this pandemic sweeps our country, thousands of us are out of school and work, stuck at home. But instead of getting trapped, we're seizing this moment to become the leaders we need. Join us at Sunrise School: an online community where we're building the skills and power we need to confront the crises we currently face."[5]

Anyone can access free classes through the Sunrise homepage, learning about online activism, acquiring new digital skills, and making connections to strengthen their professional and personal lives after the shelter-in-place orders have lifted. Even though they are locked out of the economy and will never find the security that previous generations enjoyed, these young people are filled with hope for a world reshaped by the Green New Deal—the only legislation that comes close to confronting the economic damage and amplified inequality of our post-pandemic reality.

The Sunrise Movement has shown us an alternative to the deep end, one solution for confronting the coming challenges of climate change and the economic consequences of the COVID-19 crisis. They were handed a world of inequality and catastrophe, but they did not surrender. They marched at a time when too many people in my generation snickered at their earnest protest.

Williams's Depression-era essay ended by urging the older generations to support the younger ones. He wrote:

> We can no longer ask wage earners to fight poverty single-handed. We can no longer turn our young loose in the national pastor and expect them to grow fat. We cannot consider our youth problem as one of individuals, some of

> whom will be lucky, while others will fail. We must give
> all youth its chance and to do this a certain amount of
> cooperate social action will be necessary.[6]

That is the unfulfilled legacy of the Great Depression and the Great Recession. We had a chance to treat our struggling workers with the same empathy and the same care in the twenty-first century, but we never managed to change our attitudes about wealth and poverty. With the world-altering arrival of COVID-19 and the looming threat of global warming, we must do better. Our children cannot face the challenges of the next hundred years armed only with these same misconceptions.

We need to stop pretending that failure is un-American. We must ignore the promises of politicians preaching the myth of a speedy recovery. The economic damage of COVID-19 will continue to influence our lives, our families, and our stories for decades to come. We will all experience failure and loss during the difficult days ahead. The founders of the Sunrise Movement have built these stories of shared pain into their founding charter, instead of hiding them: "We tell our stories and we honor each other's stories. We all have something to lose to climate change, and something to gain in coming together. We tell individual stories to connect with each other and understand the many different ways this crisis impacts us."[7]

Sunrise Movement activists wield personal experiences like weapons, both online and offline. In February 2019, hundreds of these young protestors filled the hallways of Republican Senate Majority Leader Mitch McConnell's office, carrying signs that read "Look me in the eyes." Those

kids solemnly lined up in the corridors of power, recount-
ing experiences with floodwaters, firestorms, and droughts.
Like the Crisis Generation, they collect stories from refugees,
victims of racial violence, Hooverville dwellers, the unemployed, Dustbowl survivors, sharecroppers, and other people
who would otherwise have been silenced.

I began this book thinking that my generation might live
up to the promise of the Crisis Generation after the Great
Recession. We did not.

The thousands of young people in the Sunrise Movement
are the real Crisis Generation. Their early work lives have
been paralyzed by COVID-19 and their economic futures
will bear the worst of post-pandemic aftershocks. But they
also conceived a mighty moonshot with the Green New
Deal, the kind of bold idea that only a generation of activists
sparked by school gun violence protests, #MeToo upheaval,
and Black Lives Matter confrontations could dream up.

These activists will enter adulthood with crushing student debt and a ruined hellscape of a job market, but they
have the crazy idea that we might be able to change the way
things are; that the world still owes us a moonshot; that we
could march, sing, and shout our stories until our government gives us what they think we deserve. And those Sunrise
Movement kids streaming into Congressional offices deserve
something better, something their parents, grandparents, and
the generations before them could not secure.

The original New Deal was equally audacious, and it
happened in a country every bit as embattled, angry, and
wounded as our own world. What can we do to be more like
them? Those are the questions that drive me now, the reason

we need to share the stories of the Crisis Generation. We can find solace as we reread these forgotten men and women from the Great Depression, but we must also rekindle the radical ideas that changed their world.

"We must give all youth its chance"[8] is a demanding goal set by Williams and his cohort of New Deal dreamers, but it is the only kind of dream worth chasing. I look at my own children, and I think about the epochal uncertainty of the pandemic and the climate change apocalypse. I hope we can follow the thread left behind by the writers of the 1930s, the people who earned the New Deal that carried us through the Great Depression. The first Crisis Generation emerged from that economic nightmare into another decade of war, but they carried our civilization safely forward with the Dust Bowl tamed, deadly diseases controlled, and World War II won.

Even as we shelter-in-place during the singular disaster of COVID-19, our contemporary standard of living would seem like science fiction to those men and women of the Great Depression; many aspects of our lives would seem more like fairy tales that you might tell to children to help them sleep through the long night. All of this was achieved against mind-boggling odds, simply because the Crisis Generation was strong enough to change things.

It all begins with stories. Stories we tell each other about a better world.

NOTES

INTRODUCTION

1. Aubrey Williams, "A Crisis for Our Youth," *The New York Times*, 19 January 1936.
2. Miguel Faria-e-Castro, "Back-of-the-Envelope Estimates of Next Quarter's Unemployment Rate | St. Louis Fed," www.stlouisfed.org, March 24, 2020, https://www.stlouisfed.org/on-the-economy/2020/march/back-envelope-estimates-next-quarters-unemployment-rate.
3. Laura Hazard Owen, "Mic Lays off Almost Everyone and Goes for a Last-Ditch Sale to Bustle," Nieman Lab, 29 November 2018, https://www.niemanlab.org/2018/11/mic-lays- off-almost-everyone-and-aims-for-a-last-ditch-sale-to-bustle/.
4. Alexis C. Madrigal, "What Happened to the Uber-for-X Companies," *The Atlantic*, 6 March 2019, https://www.theatlantic.com/technology/archive/2019/03/what-happened-uber-x-companies/584236/.
5. Alexandria Ocasio-Cortez, "Senator Markey and Representative Ocasio-Cortez Announce the Green New Deal," Facebook Watch (Senator Edward J. Markey, 7 February 2019), https:// www.facebook.com/EdJMarkey/videos/363340390918961/.
6. Ocasio-Cortez, "Senator Markey and Representative Ocasio-Cortez Announce the Green New Deal."

7. Naomi Klein, interviewed by Jon Wiener, "Naomi Klein: The Green New Deal Is Changing the Calculus of the Possible," *The Nation*, 22 February 2019, https://www.thenation.com/article/archive/naomi-klein-green-new-deal-climate-change/.

1. EDWARD NEWHOUSE

1. Edward Newhouse, *You Can't Sleep Here* (New York, Macaulay: 1934), 76.
2. "Our Lazy Writers," *The New York Times*, 19 April 1931, 53.
3. J.B Moore, *Maxwell Bodenheim* (Twayne Publishers, 1970).
4. Diana Farrell, Fiona Greig, and Amar Hamoudi, "The Online Platform Economy in 2018 | JPMorgan Chase Institute," 2018, https://institute.jpmorganchase.com/institute/research/labor-markets/report-ope-2018.htm#finding-3.
5. Newhouse, *Sleep*, 112-113.
6. Robert H. Frank, "Before Tea, Thank Your Lucky Stars," *The New York Times*, 25 April 2009, https://www.nytimes.com/2009/04/26/business/economy/26view.html.
7. Jeremy Barr, "Facebook Is Taking Over the Media Business, Vice CEO Shane Smith Says," Adage.com, May 20, 2016, https://adage.com/article/media/candid-shane-smith-sizes-vice-media-industry/304112.
8. "Trustafarian," Urban Dictionary, 2019, https://www.urban-dictionary.com/define.php?term=trustafarian.
9. Federal Writers' Project (New York, NY). 1938. *New York panorama a comprehensive view of the metropolis.* New York: Random House. http://books.google.com/books?id=lH0GAQAAIAAJ.
10. Newhouse, *Sleep*, 7.
11. Honore Balzac, *The Works of Honoré de Balzac, Volume 13*, Dana Estes (1835; repr., Boston: Dana Estes & Company, 1901), 9.
12. Stanley Kunitz, ed. *Twentieth Century Authors: A Biographical Dictionary of Modern Literature.* Supplement. (United States: H. W. Wilson, 1955), 714.

13. Scott John Hammond, *Classics of American Political and Constitutional Thought / Vol 2, Reconstruction to the Present.* (Indianapolis, Hackett 2007), 410.

14. Edward Newhouse, "Commodore Strikers Had Slaved in Basement Inferno of Heat and Speed-Up," *Daily Worker*, 18 August 1933.

15. Spencer Soper, "Inside Amazon's Warehouse," The Morning Call, September 2011, https://www.mcall.com/business/mc-xpm-2011-09-18-mc-allentown-amazon-complaints-20110917-story.html.

16. Jeff Smith, "10 Facts Retailers Don't Want You to Know About Online Shopping," Grand Rapids Institute for Information Democracy (November 26, 2012), https://griid.org/2012/11/26/10-facts-retailers-dont-want-you-to-know-about-online-shopping/.

17. Newhouse, "Commodore."

18. *Twentieth Century Authors*, 713.

19. Newhouse, "Commodore."

20. "Macaulay Employees on Strike," *Publishers Weekly*, 9 June 1994, 2144.

21. Maxwell Bodenheim, *Slow Vision* (New York: Macaulay Company, 1934), 105.

22. "Boycott Sought By Book Strikers," *The New York Times*, 20 September 1934, 25.

23. "Boycott," 25.

24. "Authors Picket Publishing House" *The New York Times*, 19 September 1934, 21.

25. "The Macaulay Ruling," 12 March 1935.

26. Joseph Freeman, "You Can Fight Here," *New Masses*, 11 December 1934, 25.

27. "Ousted Squatters See Homes Razed," *The New York Times*, 18 May 1933, 21.

28. Newhouse, *Sleep*, 247.

29. Mike Gold, "Write For Us!," *New Masses*, July 1928, 2.

30. Till von Wachter, "Challenges for the U.S. Economic Recovery," *Concurrent Resolution on the Budget Fiscal Year 2012: Hearings Before the Committee on the Budget* (United States: Government Printing Office, 2011), 402-3.

31. Wachter, "Challenges", 403.
32. Delmore Schwartz, *Once and for All : The Best of Delmore Schwartz* (New York: New Directions Publishing Corporation, 2016), 71.
33. Schwartz, *Once*, 94.
34. Schwartz, *Once*, 95.
35. Schwartz, *Once*, 71.

2. MAXWELL BODENHEIM

1. "Village Pegasus Gallops For Coins of Bourgeoise," *The Washington Post*, 22 May 1933, 2.
2. Francis Lambert McCrudden, "The Nickel Snatcher," *Raven Anthology*, No. 19 (New York: The Raven Studio), June 1935.
3. "Village," *Post*, 2.
4. *Slow*, Bodenheim, 122.
5. Ibid, 63.
6. Maxwell Bodenheim, *Slow Vision* (Macaulay Company, 1934), 209.
7. W.B Rideout, *The Radical Novel in the United States, 1900-1954: Some Interrelations of Literature and Society* (Columbia University Press, 1992), 235.
8. Dan Brown, *The Lost Symbol* (Knopf Doubleday Publishing Group, 2009), 502.
9. *Slow*, Bodenheim, 73.
10. "Frigid Wave Widespread," *The New York Times*, 30 December 1933, 1-3.
11. Maxwell Bodenheim, *Minna and Myself* (Pagan Publishing Company, 1918), 44.
12. *Slow*, Bodenheim, 41.
13. *New York Herald Tribune*, "Starvation Aid Plan Makes Real Ghost Writers, He Says." March 1935.
14. *Tribune*, "Starvation."
15. Ben Hecht, *Letters from Bohemia* (New York: Doubleday & Co, 1964).
16. Maxwell Bodenheim, *Jazz Poems*, ed. Kevin Young (Alfred A. Knopf, 2006), 39.

17. Ibid.
18. "Village Poets Pen Fence Anthology," *The New York Times*, 25 May 1936.
19. Ibid.
20. Francis Lambert McCrudden, "CROAKETTES," *Raven Anthology*, No. 30 (New York: The Raven Studio), May 1936.
21. "Poets," *Times*, 25 May 1936.
22. "The Barber of the Streets (The Street Cleaner)" No. 38 (New York: The Raven Studio), January 1937.
23. John Cabbage, *Time and Tide* (New York, Parnassus Press: 1938), 48.
24. John Locke, *Lethal People* (iUniverse: 2009), 176.
25. *New York city guide; a comprehensive guide to the five boroughs of the metropolis: Manhattan, Brooklyn, the Bronx, Queens, and Richmond* (New York: Federal Writers' Project, 1939), 128.
26. Louis Untermeyer, "A Foreward," *Minna And Myself* (New York: Pagan Publishing Company, 1918), 7-8.
27. J.B Moore, *Maxwell Bodenheim* (Twayne Publishers, 1970).
28. Maxwell Bodenheim, *Minna And Myself,* (New York: Pagan Publishing Company, 1918), 20.
29. Susan Briante, "A Letter to Eileen Myles," *Starting Today: 100 Poems for Obama's First 100 Days* (University of Iowa Press, 2010), 135.
30. Susan Briante, *Utopia Minus* (Boise, Idaho Ahsahta Press, 2011).

3. ORRICK JOHNS

1. Orrick Johns, *Time of Our Lives : The Story of My Father and Myself* (New York: Stackpole Sons, 1937), 120.
2. Ibid, 338.
3. Ibid, 323.
4. Ibid, 314.
5. Johns, *Time of Our Lives*, 316.
6. Johns, *Time*, 313.
7. Kenneth Rexroth, *Selected Poems* (New Directions, 1984), 96.
8. Johns, *Time*, 339.

9. Joseph North, *New Masses: An Anthology of the Rebel Thirties* (International Publishers, 1969), 26.

10. Granville Hicks et al., *Proletarian Literature in the United States: An Anthology* (International Publishers, 1935), 148.

11. Maxwell Bodenheim, *Advice: A Book of Poems* (A. A. Knopf, 1920), 72.

12. Ibid, 72.

13. Johns, *Time*, 344.

14. Anzia Yezierska, *Red Ribbon on a White Horse* (Persea Books, 1987), 161.

15. Yezierska, *Red*, 157.

16. Mark I. Pinsky, "Write Now," *The New Republic*, 8 December 2008, https://newrepublic.com/article/61090/write-now.

17. *New York city guide; a comprehensive guide to the five boroughs of the metropolis: Manhattan, Brooklyn, the Bronx, Queens, and Richmond* (New York: Federal Writers' Project, 1939), 50.

18. *New York City Guide*, Federal Writers Project, 129.

19. "McCoy Says Fight on Reds Cost Job," *The New York Times*, 14 February 1936, 5.

20. Jerre Mangione, *The Dream and the Deal: The Federal Writers' Project, 1935-1943* (Syracuse University Press, 1996), 187.

21. Marie Margaret Winthrop, "White Roses" *Raven Anthology* No. 11 (New York: The Raven Studio), October 1934.

22. Aubrey Williams, "A Crisis for Our Youth, *The New York Times*, 19 January 1936.

23. Ray Gustini, "Borders Group President Confirms Liquidation," *The Atlantic*, 18 July 2011, https://www.theatlantic.com/business/archive/2011/07/borders-president-confirms-liquidation/352994/.

24. Paul Constant, "Books Without Borders," *The Stranger*, 3 August 2011, https://www.thestranger.com/seattle/books-without-borders/Content?oid=9322294.

25. Dennis Johnson, "The Wrong Goodbye of Barnes and Noble," MobyLives, 7 January 2013, https://www.mhpbooks.com/the-slow-death-of-barnes-and-noble/.

26. Johns, *Time*, 348.

27. "Orrick Johns, Author, Kills Self By Poison," *The New York Times*, 9 July 1946.

28. Johns, *Time*, 352.
29. Napoleon Hill, *Think and Grow Rich : The Complete Classic Text* (New York, N.Y.: Jeremy P. Tarcher/Penguin, 2008), 15.
30. Ibid, 154.
31. Melanie Stefan, "A CV of Failures," *Nature* 468, no. 7322 (1 November 1 2010): 467–467, https://doi.org/10.1038/nj7322-467a.

4. ANCA VRBOVSKA

1. Anca Vrbovska, "Comfort," *Raven Anthology*, No. 11 (New York: The Raven Studio), October 1934.
2. *New York city guide; a comprehensive guide to the five boroughs of the metropolis: Manhattan, Brooklyn, the Bronx, Queens, and Richmond* (New York: Federal Writers' Project, 1939), 140.
3. Anca Vrbovska, *The Gate Beyond the Sun: New and Selected Poems* (New York, New Orlando Publications. 1970).
4. Vrbovska, "Autumn Wind," *Raven*, December 1933.
5. "Dear Ravens," Francis McCrudden, *Raven Anthology* (New York: The Raven Studio), January 1934
6. Vrbovska, "Skyscraper," *Raven*, November 1934.
7. "What's Occupying Wall Street?," *The Wall Street Journal*, 17 October 2011, sec. Opinion, https://www.wsj.com/articles/SB10001424052970203499704576625302455112990.
8. Todd Gitlin, "The Left Declares Its Independence," *The New York Times*, 8 October 2011, sec. Opinion, https://www.nytimes.com/2011/10/09/opinion/sunday/occupy-wall-street-and-the-tea-party.html.
9. Anne H. Soukhanov, "Word Watch," *The Atlantic*, 1 April 1997, https://www.theatlantic.com/magazine/archive/1997/04/word-watch/376847/.
10. Mandy Henk, "Occupy Libraries: Guerrilla Librarianship for the People," Occupy Wall Street Library, 28 October 2011, https://peopleslibrary.wordpress.com/2011/10/28/occupy-libraries-guerrilla-librarianship-for-the-people/.
11. McCrudden, *Raven*, August 1934.

12. "CAPITALS MISSING IN POEM SHOW HERE;
    Original Spelling Also Finds Favor in Verse Displayed in
    Washington Square," *The New York Times*, 21 May 21 1934.

13. "TACKS GONE, TACT SAVES POEM SHOW;
    Washington Sq. Display Disrupted After Rain as Authors
    Hunt Lost Fasteners." *The New York Times*, 22 May 1934.

14. Ross Wetzsteon, *Republic of Dreams: Greenwich Village: The
    American Bohemia, 1910-1960* (Simon & Schuster, 2007), 330.

15. Joe Gould, "His Religion," *Raven*, November 1934.

16. Jack Alexander, *St. Louis Post-Dispatch*, 5 August 1934, Page 51.

17. "VILLAGE PRINCE GETS JAIL TERM," *Los Angeles
    Times* 18 April 1924;

18. "GIRL, 18, VANISHES WITH BOGUS PRINCE," *The
    New York Times*, 18 June 1934.

19. *New York City Guide*, Federal Writers Project, 140-141.

20. Alexander, *Post-Dispatch*, 5 August 1934, Page 51.

21. "Missing Poet and Her 'Count' Found, Jailed" *New York
    Tribune*, 18 June 1934.

22. McCrudden, *Raven*, September 1934.

23. Vincente Beltrone, "Prospective Villagers," *Raven*, October
    1934.

24. Louise Krist, "Mood in Ebony," *Raven*, August 1935.

25. Vrbovska, "Winds and Clouds," *Raven*, July 1935.

26. Vrbovska, "Vacation Reverie," *Raven*, October 1935.

27. Margaret Egri, "Goethe's Dream of Death," *Raven*,
    December 1935.

28. Ralph E. Renaud, "Pegasus Snorted," *The Washington Post*, 1
    June 1935.

29. Francis Lambert McCrudden, *Raven Anthology*, No. 24 (New
    York: The Raven Studio), November 1935.

30. Vrbovska, "Impression," *Raven*, January 1936.

31. Anca Vrbovska, "The Proud White Rose," *Raven Anthology*,
    No. 37 (New York: The Raven Studio), December 1936.

32. May Swenson and Anca Vrbovska, "Czechoslovakian
    Lore," New York City, New York, 1938. Manuscript/Mixed
    Material. https://www.loc.gov/item/wpalh001610/.

33. R. R. Knudson and Suzzanne Bigelow, *May Swenson: A Poet's Life in Photos* (Logan, Utah: Utah State University Press, 1996), 43.

34. May Swenson and Iriving Fajans, "Lore of Department Store Workers," New York City, New York, 1939. PDF. https://www.loc.gov/item/wpalh001612/.

35. Ibid.

36. May Swenson and L Hammer, *May Swenson: Collected Poems (LOA \#239)* (Library of America, 2013).

37. R. R. Knudson, *The Wonderful Pen of May Swenson* (New York: Macmillan Publishing Company, 1992), 55.

38. Ibid, 56.

39. Vrbovska, "Sanguine Sea" *The Gate Beyond the Sun: New and Selected Poems.* New York, New Orlando Publications. 1970.

40. "Biography - Vrbovska, Anca (1905-1989)," *Gale Literature: Contemporary Authors,* www.gale.com.

41. Nikil Saval, *Cubed: A Secret History of the Workplace* (Knopf Doubleday Publishing Group, 2014), 115.

42. Daniel J. Leab, *A Union of Individuals: The Formation of the American Newspaper Guild* (New York: Columbia University Press, 1970), 46.

43. "La Guardia Enjoys Spotlight At Benefit," *The New York Times,* 30 March 1935.

44. Leab, *Union,* 114.

45. "Guild Still Picketing," *The New York Times,* 26 August 1934, 17.

46. Edward Newhouse, "The First Big Guild Strike," *New Masses,* 27 November 1934, 8-10.

47. "Guild Is Blamed As L. I. Star Quits," *The New York Times,* 26 June 1938, 14.

5. CORNELL WOOLRICH

1. Francis M Nevins, *Cornell Woolrich: First You Dream, Then You Die* (New York: Mysterious Press, 1988), 76.

2. Cornell Woolrich and M.T Bassett, *Blues of a Lifetime: Autobiography of Cornell Woolrich* (University of Wisconsin Press, 1991), 70.

3. Ibid, 93.
4. William L. Silber, "Why Did FDR's Bank Holiday Succeed?," papers.ssrn.com (Rochester, NY, August 1, 2007), 20.
5. Horace Gregory, *The House on Jefferson Street: A Cycle of Memories* (Holt, Rinehart and Winston, 1971).
6. Woolrich, *Blues*, 70.
7. "Kissless Bride Quits Writer," *Los Angeles Times*, 23 April 1933.
8. Woolrich, *Blues*, 91.
9. Cornell Woolrich, *Darkness at Dawn: Early Suspense Classics* (Southern Illinois University Press, 1985), 1.
10. Cornell Woolrich, *Nightwebs: A Collection of Stories* (Victor Gollancz, 1974), 407.
11. Woolrich, *Darkness*, 236.
12. "A.B.A. Convention," *Publishers Weekly*, 18 January 1936, 203.
13. "New Year Price War on Books Freed From Code," *Publishers Weekly*, 5 January 1935, 48.
14. Pascal-Emmanuel Gobry, "How Amazon Makes Money From The Kindle - Business Insider," *Business Insider*, 18 October 2011, https://www.businessinsider.com/kindle-economics-2011-10.
15. "Consumers Sue Apple, Publishers Alleging E-Book Price Fixing | Hagens Berman | National Class Action Litigation Firm Based in Seattle, WA," www.hbsslaw.com, 9 August 2011.
16. "Justice Department Reaches Settlement with Macmillan in E-Books Case," www.justice.gov, 8 February 2013, https://www.justice.gov/opa/pr/justice-department-reaches-settle-ment-macmillan-e-books-case.
17. Jillian D'Onfro, "Hachette Authors Write A Letter To Amazon's Board: Do You, Personally, Want To Be Associated With This War?," *Business Insider*, 15 September 2014, https://www.businessinsider.com/hachette-authors-united-write-to-amazon-board-2014-9.
18. Hayley Tsukayama, "Amazon, Hachette Reach Agreement in Book Dispute," *The Washington Post*, 13 November 2014, https://www.

washingtonpost.com/news/the-switch/wp/2014/11/13/
amazon-hachette-reach-agreement-in-book-dispute/.

19. Ursula Le Guin, "Ursula Le Guin," YouTube, 20 November 2014, https://www.youtube.com/watch?v=Et9Nf-rsALk&-feature=
emb_title.

20. "Price-Fixing Books Returned By Store; Publisher Accepts Macy Offer of 36,000 Unsold Copies of 'Gone With the Wind,'" *The New York Times*, 24 March 1937, 46.

21. Ibid.

22. Woolrich, "Dead on Her Feet," *Darkness*, 219.

23. Woolrich, "One and a Half Murders," *Nightwebs*, 315.

24. Ibid, 316-317.

25. Dennis Lehane, *Moonlight Mile* (William Morrow, 2010), 18.

26. Ibid, 211.

27. Woolrich, "Death in the Air," *Nightwebs*, 252.

28. Ibid, 255.

29. Ibid, 250.

30. Edward Weeks, "Hard Times and the Author," *Atlantic Monthly*, May 1935, 559.

31. Ibid, 561.

32. Herbert W. Howill, "News and Views on Literary London," *The New York Times*, 31 October 1937, 104.

33. James Dourgarian, "Armed Service Editions," Abaa.org, accessed 18 February 2020, https://www.abaa.org/members-articles/armed-service-editions.

34. Mark Coker, "2019 Book Industry Predictions: The Butterflies Will Flap Their Wings," Smashwords, December 2018, https://blog.smashwords.com/2018/12/2019-book-industry-predictions.html.

35. Napoleon Hill, *Think and Grow Rich : The Complete Classic Text* (New York, N.Y.: Jeremy P. Tarcher/Penguin, 2008), 81.

36. Steve Lohr, "In Case You Wondered, a Real Human Wrote This Column," *The New York Times*, 10 September 2011.

37. "Badgers Blow Away UNLV, 51-17," Big Ten Network, 2 September 2011, https://btn.com/2011/09/01/wisconsin-blows-away-unlv-51-17/.

38. Alex Hern, "New AI Fake Text Generator May Be Too Dangerous to Release, Say Creators," *The Guardian*, 15 February 2019.

39. Alec Radford and Jeffrey Wu, et. al., "Better Language Models and Their Implications," *OpenAI*, 14 February 2019, https://openai.com/blog/better-language-models/

40. Ibid.

41. Marshall Brain, "Robots in 2015, by Marshall Brain," marshallbrain.com, 2003, http://marshallbrain.com/robots-in-2015.htm.

42. "Press-a-Button Counter-Revolution," *New Masses*, 11 September 1934, 12-14.

7. MURIEL RUKEYSER

1. Muriel Rukeyser, *Theory of Flight* (New Haven: Yale University Press, 1935), 49.

2. Ibid, 13.

3. "Authors Protest Lack of WPA Aid," *The New York Times*, 30 December 1935, 17.

4. Muriel Rukeyser, *Out of Silence: Selected Poems* (Evanston: TriQuarterly Books, 1994), 17.

5. Ibid, 20

6. David J. Wishart, *Encyclopedia of the Great Plains* (Lincoln: University of Nebraska Press, 2004), 276.

7. Muriel Rukeyser, *The Collected Poems* (McGraw-Hill, 1979), 75.

8. Rukeyser, *Silence*, 46.

9. "Women Here To Aid Loyalists In Spain," *The New York Times*, 22 November 1936, 39.

10. "Mediterranean," *New Masses*, 14 September 1937, 19.

11. Adrienne Rich, *What Is Found There: Notebooks on Poetry and Politics (Expanded Edition)* (New York: W. W. Norton, 2003), 100-101.

12. "Mediterranean," *New Masses*, 20.

13. "Park Sitters Shun Open-Air Library," *The New York Times*, 18 August 1935, 78.

14. Ibid.
15. "Google Checks Out Library Books," Google Press, 14 December 2004, http://googlepress.blogspot.com/2004/12/google-checks-out-library-books.html.
16. John Hudson, "Judge Rejects Google Books Arrangement With the Authors' Guild," *The Atlantic*, 22 March 2011, https://www.theatlantic.com/technology/archive/2011/03/judge-rejects-googles-settlement-authors-guPageild/348986/.
17. "Authors Guild v. Google, Part II: Fair Use Proceedings," Electronic Frontier Foundation, 7 November 2013, https://www.eff.org/cases/authors-guild-v-google-part-ii-fair-use-proceedings.
18. Scott Dougall, "A Change to Our Retailer Partner Program: EBooks Resellers to Wind Down Next Year," Google Books, 11 April 2011, http://booksearch.blogspot.com/2012/04/change-to-our-retailer-partner-program.html .
19. "OPEN LETTER TO LIBRARIANS," HarperCollins Publishers, 1 March 2011, https://www.harpercollins.com/corporate/press-releases/open-letter-to-librarians/.
20. Ursula Le Guin, "Ursula Le Guin," YouTube Video, YouTube, 20 November 2014, https://www.youtube.com/watch?v=Et9Nf-rsALk&feature=emb_title.
21. Andrew Albanese, "Publisher, Author Groups Protest Library Book Scanning Program," *Publishers Weekly*, 14 February 2019, https://www.publishersweekly.com/pw/by-topic/industry-news/libraries/article/79262-could-library-book-scanning-be-headed-back-to-court.html .

8. NATHANAEL WEST

1. Nathanael West, *Novels and Other Writings* (New York: Library of America, 1997), 777.
2. Dashiell Hammett, *The Thin Man* (New York: Knopf Doubleday Publishing Group, 2011), 151.
3. Nathanael West, *Miss Lonelyhearts & the Day of the Locust* (Cambridge, MA: New Directions, 2009), 22.

4. "Liveright, Inc, Put Into Bankruptcy," *The New York Times*, 5 May 1933, 16.
5. Sarah Weinman, "Norton Relaunches Liveright & Company Imprint," *Publishers Lunch*, 21 June 2011, https://lunch.publishersmarketplace.com/2011/06/people-etc-2/.
6. D.H Lawrence, *Introductions and Reviews* (Cambridge, UK: Cambridge University Press, 2005), 119.
7. "Long Island Towns Still Snowbound," *New York Times*, 22 February 1934, 3.
8. West, *Writings*, 745.
9. Nathanael West, *The Dream Life Of Balso Snell & A Cool Million: Two Novels* (New York : Farrar, Straus and Giroux, 1931-34), 177.
10. May Swenson and Irving Fajans, *Irving Fajans* (New York, NY), Manuscript/Mixed Material. https://www.loc.gov/item/wpalh001613/.
11. Eileen Myles, "Anonymous," *Occupy Wall Street Poetry Anthology* https://peopleslibrary.files.wordpress.com/2011/11/ows-poetry-anthology4.pdf.
12. We Are the 99 Percent, Tumblr, 15 September 2012, https://wearethe99percent.tumblr.com/post/31567195495/i-am-a-30-year-old-software-engineer-with-vast.
13. We Are the 99 Percent, Tumblr, 11 November 2011, https://wearethe99percent.tumblr.com/post/12639892423/i-am-a-27-year-old-veteran-of-the-iraq-war-i.
14. Stephen Boyer and Filip Marinovich, eds., *Occupy Wall Street Poetry Anthology* https://peopleslibrary.files.wordpress.com/2011/11/ows-poetry-anthology4.pdf.
15. Stuart Leonard, "Taking Brooklyn Bridge," *Occupy*, https://peopleslibrary.files.wordpress.com/2011/11/ows-poetry-anthology4.pdf.
16. Terence Degnan, *Occupy*, https://peopleslibrary.files.wordpress.com/2011/11/ows-poetry-anthology4.pdf.
17. Stephen Boyer, "Occupy Wall St. Poetry Update," Occupy Wall Street Library, 23 October 2011, https://peopleslibrary.wordpress.com/2011/10/22/occupy-wall-st-poetry-update/.

18. "Citi Debuts New National Advertising Campaign for U.S. Citi Cards," Citigroup, 29 October 2007, https://www.citi-group.com/citi/news/2007/071030c.htm .
19. Ibid.
20. Michael Lewis, *The Big Short: Inside the Doomsday Machine* (New York: W. W. Norton, 2011), 261.

9. RICHARD WRIGHT

1. Walter B. Rideout, *The Radical Novel in the United States* (Cambridge, MA: Harvard University Press, 1956), 243.
2. Ibid, 240.
3. Richard Wright, "I Have Seen Black Hands," *New Masses,* 26 June 1936.
4. Joseph North, "Title Page," in *New Masses: An Anthology of the Rebel Thirties*, ed. Joseph North (New York: International Publishers, 1969), 34.
5. Ibid, 348.
6. "Novelists Strike Fails To Affect Nation Whatsoever," *The Onion*, 15 March 2008, https://entertainment.theonion.com/novelists-strike-fails-to-affect-nation-whatsoever-1819569689.
7. Ibid.
8. Richard Wright, *Black Boy* (New York: Harper Perennial Modern Classics, 2009), 264.
9. Richard Wright, "Joe Louis Uncovers Dynamite," *New Masses*, 8 October 1935.
10. Scott Lucas, "Occupy Wall Street 1st-Hand: 'All Around Me, Peaceful Protesters Were Being Pepper-Sprayed and Zip-Cuffed' (Harkinson)," EA World View, 15 November 2011, http://www.enduringamerica.com/home/2011/11/15/occupy-wall-street-1st-hand-all-around-me-peaceful-protester.html.
11. Richard Wright, *Uncle Tom's Children* (New York: HarperCollins, 2009), 145
12. Ernest Hemingway, "Appendix 1," *For Whom the Bell Tolls: The Hemingway Library Edition* (New York: Scribner, 2019), 479.

13. Hazel Rowley, *Richard Wright: The Life and Times* (New York: Henry Holt and Company, 2002), 129.

14. Elise Robinson, "Federal Writers Project Has Become Just A Hobo's Haven, Says Commentator," *Minneapolis Star Tribune*, 16 March 1938.

15. Federal Writers' Project, *New York Panorama: A Comprehensive View of the Metropolis, Presented in a Series of Articles Prepared by the Federal Writers' Project of the Works Progress Administration in New York City* (New York: Random House, 1938), 146.

16. Ibid, 141.

17. Ibid, 142.

18. Harry Roskolenko, *When I Was Last on Cherry Street* (New York Stein and Day, 1965), 154.

19. Ibid.

20. "Winner of Story Magazine's National Prize Contest for WPA Writers," *New Masses*, 10 May 1938, 125.

21. S. Funaroff and Willard Maas, "The Editors," *New Masses*, 10 May 1938, 97.

22. Monty Noam Penkower, *The Federal Writers' Project: a Study in Government Patronage of the Arts* (Champaign: University of Illinois Press, 1977).

23. Penkower, *Federal*, 174.

24. Richard Wright, *American Stuff: An Anthology of Prose & Verse by Members of the Federal Writers' Project*, Federal Writers' Project and Federal Art Project (New York: The Viking press, 1937), 51.

25. Andrew Bruce Davidson, *Book of Job* (Cambridge, UK: Cambridge University Press, 1884), 169.

26. Richard Wright, *How "Bigger" Was Born: The Story of Native Son* (New York: Harper & Brothers, 1940), xlii.

27. Ibid.

28. Richard Wright, *Native Son* (New York: HarperCollins, 1940), 14.

29. Hazel Rowley, *Richard Wright: The Life and Times* (New York: Henry Holt and Company, 2002), 152.

30. Wright, *Native*, 98.

10. EDWARD NEWHOUSE & THE CRISIS GENERATION

1. Stanley Kunitz, ed., *Twentieth Century Authors: A Biographical Dictionary of Modern Literature* (New York: H. W. Wilson, 1955), 714.
2. Edward Newhouse, *This Is Your Day* (New York: L. Furman, 1937), 39.
3. "Anti-Red Writers Barred From WPA Witness Declares," *The New York Times*, 16 September 1938, 16.
4. Jerre Mangione, *The Dream and the Deal: The Federal Writers' Project, 1935-1943* (Syracuse: Syracuse University Press, 1996), 188.
5. S. Funaroff, "In Conclusion," *New Masses*, 10 May 1938, 127.
6. Maxwell Bodenheim, "Feminist," *New Masses*, 10 May 1938, 112.
7. Funaroff, "Conclusion," *Masses*, 127.
8. "Winner of Story Magazine's National Prize Contest for WPA Writers," *New Masses*, 10 May 1938, 125.
9. Funaroff, "Conclusion," *Masses*, 127.
10. "Testimony Cited on WPA Book Bias," *The New York Times*, 27 November 1938, 31.
11. Jason Boog, "In Face of NEA Cuts, Small Presses Worry About Their Futures," *Publishers Weekly*, 16 March 2017, https://www.publishersweekly.com/pw/by-topic/indus-try-news/publisher-news/article/73085-in-face-of-nea-cuts-small-presses-worry-about-their-futures.html .
12. Edward Newhouse, "My Life With Clara Bow," *The New Yorker*, 25 September 1936, 36.
13. Federal Writers Project, *Los Angeles in the 1930s: The WPA Guide to the City of Angels* (Berkeley: University of California Press, 2011), 231.
14. Ibid, 12.

CONCLUSION

1. Aubrey Williams, "A Crisis for Our Youth," *The New York Times*, 19 January 1936.

2. Varshini Prakash, "Sunrise Livestream Watch Party,"
    YouTube, 19 September 2017, https://www.youtube.com/
    watch?v=WL5134-QV7I&t=1148s

3. Ibid.

4. Sophie Geoghegan, "'Rapid, Far-Reaching and
    Unprecedented Changes' Are Vital to Limit Global Warming
    to 1.5°C - EIA," Environmental Investigation Agency,
    8 October 2018, https://eia-international.org/blog/rap-
    id-far-reaching-unprecedented- changes-vital-limit-glob-
    al-warming-1-5c/ .

5. "Come to Sunrise School," Sunrise Movement, April 2020,
    https://www.sunrisemovement.org/sunrise-school.

6. Williams, "Crisis," *Times*, January 19, 1936.

7. "Our Principles," Sunrise Movement, https://www.sun-
    risemovement.org/principles

8. Williams, "Crisis," *Times*, January 19, 1936.

ACKNOWLEDGEMENTS

I am so grateful for OR Books' support throughout the life of this manuscript. I especially need to thank Colin Robinson, Justin Humphries, Emma Ingrisani, and Susan Rella for their edits. In addition, a few magazine editors helped me shape some of these stories. I need to thank Ed Park and Andrew Leland for editing "Bohemian Rhapsody" at *The Believer*; Travis Nichols and Catherine Halley for editing "And Wow He Died As Wow He Lived" at *The Poetry Foundation*; Jonathan Hahn for editing "The Irretrievable Cent of Fate" at *The Los Angeles Review of Books*; Steve Charles for editing "Sad Men" at *Wabash Magazine*; Matt Buchanan for editing "Belabored Empires" at *The Awl*, and Parul Sehgal for editing "The DOJ E-Book Lawsuit: Is It 1934 All Over Again?" at *NPR Books*.

A number of wonderful libraries and researchers guided my research journey, including David A. Taylor, Robert Boynton, Mitchell Stephens, Lawrence Weschler, Brooke Kroeger, Michael Sweeney, Alison Dinsmore, and many others. A special thanks to the epic collections at the New York Historical Museum & Library, the Tamiment Library & Robert F. Wagner Labor Archives, the Riazanov Library, Marxists.org, the Library of Congress, Los Angeles Public

Library, and the New York Public Library for providing access to their materials.

Early in this project, Andrew Kessler let me host a Raven Poetry Circle-style reading in his pop-up bookstore, Ed's Martian Book. A few wonderful people supported that project, including friends like Sarah Weinman, Marc Eliot Stein, Elizabeth Keenan, Rachel Kramer Bussel, Guy LeCharles Gonzalez, Susan Deford, Lisa Dierbeck, and Edward Champion. Thanks to Justin Bozung, Craig Morgan Teicher, Pual Malmont, and Jeffry Yamaguchi for all your supportive conversations along the way.

Finally, thanks to Caitlin, Olive, and Otto for sharing all my stories.

© *Caitlin Shamberg*

Jason Boog is the West Coast correspondent for *Publishers Weekly* and was previously publishing editor at *Mediabistro*, leading the *GalleyCat* and *AppNewser* blogs. He is the author of *Born Reading: Bringing Up Bookworms in a Digital Age*. His journalism has appeared in *The Believer*, *Salon*, *The Awl*, *NPR Books*, and *The Los Angeles Review of Books*.

CPSIA information can be obtained
at www.ICGtesting.com
Printed in the USA
JSHW020728161021
19611JS00001B/78